Two weeks in May 1945

Sandbostel Concentration Camp

and the

Friends Ambulance Unit

Clifford Barnard

Quaker Home Service
1999

First published 1999 by Quaker Home Service, Friends House,
173–177 Euston Road, London NW1 2BJ

http://www. quaker. org. uk

ISBN O 85245 315 9

Cover design: Jon Sargent

Design and layout: Curlew Productions, Kelso TD5 8PD, Scotland

Printed by
Warwick Printing Company, Warwick CV34 4DR

*To those nameless, unknown
hundreds who spent the last
days of their lives in this
terrible place*

The author, February 1945, while on 48 hours' leave in Brussels

Contents

Foreword

Last year, when Clifford Barnard asked me to read in draft form his book about the liberation of Sandbostel Concentration Camp, I was happy to do so out of friendship and respect. I was born in 1944, and have as much awareness of the atrocities of Nazism as any other reasonably educated British person. But nothing could have prepared me for the personal, detailed account that Clifford's book quietly and unsensationally gives. Clifford is an essentially modest man, just as the Friends Ambulance Unit in its meticulously recorded history is essentially modest, and it is a deep irony to find, in times when the graphic representation of violence is integral to our media, that quiet exact recording makes the greatest impact.

At times, as Paul Fussell noted in *The Great War and Modern Memory* (Oxford: Oxford University Press, 1975), the ordinary language of story-telling cannot cope with the extremity of human experience, and Clifford resorts to expedients such as the passive voice: 'The concentration camp was entered … The dreadful work was started … Huts were cleansed …' He also gives us lists: diet sheets, schedules of equipment etc., which are all the more telling for their spareness.

After the initial horror came the work of caring for the liberated. The FAU, together with army medical personnel and local women, saw to the washing and delousing and basic health needs of the half–dead prisoners in a way that is reminiscent of a biblical tale. Typhus was an ever–present danger, and the shelling from the nearly defeated German army had not yet stopped. Phrases like 'continuing till well after midnight' give hints of the uncalculated self–giving that was involved. Again, Clifford's restraint is telling. Grief was an integral part of the process; grief most of all at 'lives [that] could not be saved, and others whose hurts could not be healed'.

Perhaps the most remarkable aspect of Clifford's account is the contact he made in 1997 via an advertisement in a Bremen newspaper with nine of the German women who were drafted in to help with the 1945 operation. All gave intensely moving accounts. Uncertain about the nature of the work, fearful that they might themselves be subjected to some kind of atrocity, these women were assured of safety both by the Allied army personnel and by the Friends Ambulance Unit, and thereafter worked 'without restraint to the point of exhaustion'. 'In the Hitler Youth,' said one, 'we had heard only of the good and noble things and our belief was deeply shattered.' Another remembered a soldier called Joseph, in another almost biblical gesture, actually giving her his own shoes. One woman finished her letter to Clifford thus: 'Such things must never, ever be allowed to happen again anywhere in the world.'

This is the undoubted message of *Two Weeks in May*: the memorial phrase, 'Lest we forget'. But Clifford also gives us the religious foundation for his own and FAU's work. In 1943, aged eighteen, having met the conditions of his tribunal to be a registered conscientious objector to fighting in the war, he sat on a hillside in the Mendips and realised that 'I knew God to the extent that I know myself at that moment. There is only one value, one reality, life. I must try to be great enough in spirit to help others show love to the whole world, like those who have shown me love.' Quakers, or Friends, have no creed. They find God where life is, where love is. Clifford's account of the liberation of Sandbostel demonstrates that even in the degradation of the concentration camps, among the lice, the excrement, amongst disease and death and evidence of almost unspeakable human atrocity, God can be found.

Alison Leonard

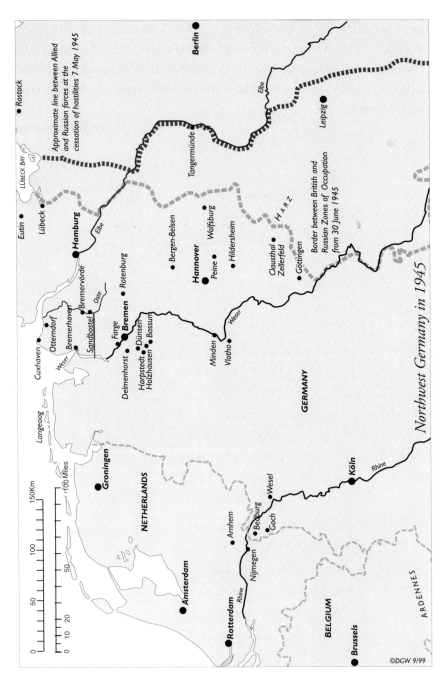

Northwest Germany in 1945

Berlin

Rostock

Leipzig

LÜBECK BAY

Approximate line between Allied
and Russian forces at the
cessation of hostilities 7 May 1945

Eutin

Lübeck

Elbe

Tangermünde

Hamburg

Bergen-Belsen

Wolfsburg

Hannover

Peine

Hildersheim

HARZ

Clausthal
Zellerfeld

Göttingen

Border between British and
Russian Zones of Occupation
from 30 June 1945

Rotenburg

Bremervörde

Oste

Elbe

Otterndorf

Bremerhaven

Sandbostel

Farge

Bremen

Dünsen

Bassum

Cuxhaven

Weser

Delmenhorst

Harpstedt

Holzhausen

Minden

Vlotho

Weser

GERMANY

Langeoog

Groningen

Köln

Rhine

NETHERLANDS

Wesel

Bedburg

Goch

Arnhem

Nijmegen

Rhine

Amsterdam

Rotterdam

BELGIUM

Brussels

ARDENNES

150Km

100

50

100 Miles

50

20

10

0

©DGW 9/99

Abbreviations

BRC	British Red Cross
BGH	British General Hospital
CAD	Civilian Affairs Detachment of the British Army
CCS	Casualty Clearing Station
CO	Conscientious Objector
COBSRA	Council of British Societies for Relief Abroad
DP	Displaced Person
ENSA	Entertainments National Services Association
FAU	Friends Ambulance Unit
FDS	Field Dressing Station
FRS	Friends Relief Service
Lt Fd Amb	Light Field Ambulance
Mil Gov Det	Military Government Detachment
OR	Other Rank
PoW	Prisoner of War
RAMC	Royal Army Medical Corps
REME	Royal Electrical and Mechanical Engineers
SS	Schutzstaffel, a paramilitary organisation within the Nazi Party that provided Hitler's bodyguard, security forces and concentration camp guards
UNRRA	United Nations Relief and Rehabilitation Administration
VE Day	Victory in Europe Day

Preface

Why write another book about the Holocaust? Why drag up atrocities of over fifty years ago when we have had Bosnia, Cambodia and Rwanda in more recent times, and now, as I write, Kosovo? Surely, it is time to bury the past and let it lie? These and other questions went through my mind when I was considering writing this book, and I feel they need answering.

The first stirring came when Lyn Smith, a Sound Archivist at the Imperial War Museum in London, addressed the Friends Ambulance Unit reunion at York in November 1996 about her forthcoming book *Pacifists in Action: The Experience of the Friends Ambulance Unit in the Second World War* (York: Sessions, 1998) and sought help from members on their experiences. While writing a few brief notes for her on the events at Sandbostel it became clear to me that here was a story that was still relevant and one that should be told more fully. Little about Sandbostel has been published anywhere in English. The older members of 2 FAU, of the relief section of which I was a member, were sadly no longer with us, so maybe I should tackle it.

I was also struck by some words of David Blamires in his review of Grigor McClelland's book *Embers of War: Letters from a Quaker Relief*

Worker in War–torn Germany in the *Friends Quarterly,* October 1997, where he wrote: 'It is important for us to have these and other personal records of life during these periods of war, persecution, deprivation and stress. It is to be hoped that other Friends have diaries or letters that will help later generations to begin to understand some of the national and personal traumas that characterise the twentieth century.' I remembered that my father had kept all my letters home from my time in the Friends Ambulance Unit, covering four and a half years. I retrieved them from very dusty files in my loft, and read them for the first time since I had written them. I found three letters from my time at Sandbostel.

A few years earlier Dennis Wickham's diary had come into my possession following his death. Dennis was deputy section leader of 2 FAU at the time, and wrote his diary daily. I can still picture him last thing at night scribbling in an old exercise book, sitting on the edge of a bunk, in a tent, or in a sleeping bag on the floor, whatever we had been through that day or whatever the conditions we were in. Then, on writing to the remaining members of the team of my intention to write up our experiences at Sandbostel, I discovered that both Gordon Taylor and Hugh Johnes had written memoirs for their families of their times soon after returning home. Of the thirteen members of 2 FAU at the time, I found that four had sadly died. Three I was unable to trace and another two did not reply to my letter, but I had three very helpful replies to augment Dennis's diary and my own letters, together with the official reports of the British Army units involved.

Several people to whom I had talked about these experiences encouraged me to set it down before it was too late. But after more than fifty years it is not desirable, or even possible, to write a book of this nature from memory alone. There is a freshness and immediacy about recording things at the time, and I am glad to have been able to find and collect together these contemporary letters, diaries, memoirs, articles and reports. I have quoted at some length from these various sources to tell the story rather than relying on my own memory of the events.

But there is a deeper purpose in writing this book, perhaps not well defined: we need to know the truth so that the past can be laid to rest. Stevie Krayer, referring to the Papon trial in France, has said it is about justice. In a letter to *The Friend,* 7 November 1997, she went on to say, 'it is also about the relevance of the past to the present and indeed the future. The accused no longer say, "I was only obeying orders" – these days they say, "Holocaust? What Holocaust?"'.

Although a substantial part is not described in my own words, apart from the extracts from my own letters home, this book is the record of events which I personally witnessed. I hope it will become another small piece of the documented evidence that will be increasingly important to counter those who would deny or excuse the atrocities committed by the Nazis. I agree with Harry Albright when he wrote in an editorial in *The Friend,* 17 October 1997, 'we owe it to all who suffered and died at their hands, and to future generations who might suffer again, never to let that happen.'

This book is not a detailed history of Sandbostel. This has been most adequately done, although in German, by Werner Borgsen and Klaus Volland in *Stalag XB Sandbostel: zur Geschichte eines Kriegsgefangenen–und KZ–Auffanglagers in Norddeutschland 1939–1945* (Bremen: Edition Temmen, 1991). What I have tried to compile is the story of a rescue operation from personal viewpoints; facts and figures from official sources have been used only where necessary to complete the picture.

Those wishing to read more about the medical conditions that had to be confronted and the treatments that were pursued are referred to a very full account by Lieutenant -Colonel F.S. Fiddes, RAMC, who was the Commanding Officer of 10 Casualty Clearing Station in *Report on Sandbostel May 1945,* written and printed in the field, August 1945, by the Company Office, 10 CCS. This has not been published but is included in the archives in the Department of Documents at the Imperial War Museum in London.

Prologue

Before I start my account of FAU work in Europe, it is perhaps appropriate to give some explanation of how I became a conscientious objector in the first place. My parents were both Quakers and pacifists. They provided a caring and loving home atmosphere where I gradually absorbed much of their outlook on life. I knew at an early age that I could not kill. At about eleven years of age a playmate lent me his airgun, without my parents' knowledge, and searching around the garden for a target I shot and killed a blue tit. I was filled with remorse at the little life I had so wantonly destroyed and the guilt stayed with me for many days.

At about the same age I was sent to St Christopher School, a progressive, vegetarian, co-educational school at Letchworth in Hertfordshire. Although not one of the Friends' schools, it was run by a Quaker couple, Lyn and Eleanor Harris. Lyn had been in prison during the First World War as a conscientious objector, and many of the staff were also pacifists. Lyn Harris's weekly talk on current affairs to the senior pupils and the general way in which most lessons were presented encouraged us children to take an interest in the world and its problems and to be socially responsible. The staff were generally kind and helpful and often became known on first-name terms. It was all very democratic, the children, through a council and school meetings, having a say in how the school was run. I was happy and readily absorbed the prevailing air of tolerance to every view. I found it gentle, and there was certainly no hint of pacifist indoctrination.

I was much influenced by a book that came into my hands at this time, Vera Brittain's *Humiliation with Honour*,[2] where, in a series of letters to her son and daughter who had been evacuated to Canada, she explains her attitudes to war. Her daughter was later to become known as Shirley Williams, the Liberal Democrat politician. I had also read with great interest the writings of several Friends and was aware of the historic Quaker peace testimony and its long heritage of witness to peace and reconciling diplomacy. I came to admire many individual Quaker attempts to live in 'that life and power that takes away the occasion of all wars'.[3] For them, pacifism was not a negative attitude of simply being against war, but was a whole way of living that avoided contributing in any way, or getting into situations where war seemed to be the only solution. I came to see that, even against something as evil as Hitler, war was not an option, everything must be tried first, for, once hostilities began, rational thinking seemed to go out of the window. So I came to register as a conscientious objector. It was a far from easy decision, going against the prevailing attitudes of my peer group, but it was one I came to feel I had to make. Only one other boy in my year thought as I did. Despite my religious illiteracy and immature spirituality I came to believe that war and preparation for war were inconsistent with the way Jesus had lived his life.

While still at school in January 1943, and shortly before my eighteenth birthday, I had to go before a Tribunal which considered my application to be registered as a conscientious objector. This was held at the County Court at Bloomsbury in London, where Judge David Davies and two laymen questioned me. I remember it as a difficult occasion. The three applicants before me were turned down and appeared to be heading for prison. However, much to my relief I was given exemption from military service on condition that I undertook full-time hospital or ambulance work under civilian control. This allowed me to fulfil my wish to join the Friends Ambulance Unit, whose exploits I had followed with great interest, and which had already accepted me pending the outcome of the Tribunal.

I left school in early July 1943 as soon as I had completed my Higher School Certificate exams. As there was not an FAU training camp until mid-September, I met the conditions of the Tribunal by working as an orderly at Winford Orthopaedic Hospital, near Bristol, with a group of other conscientious objectors. The following extract from a letter home, while at Winford, may give some idea of my thinking at the age of eighteen.

> Just lately I have been thinking about my attitude to religion, because after all it is the main reason why I am here. I have been worried why I never consciously pray. I usually just sit and think quietly when I have something on my mind. Recently with an afternoon off I went up into the Mendip Hills, and with a splendid view before me and such quietness around me, I sat down on a grassy bank and started to think. Suddenly, it came to me that I don't formally pray,

because I do not think it right or profitable to ask God that He arranges the universe for me. I realised then that I knew God to the extent that I know myself at that moment. God is the inward spark that if necessary will persuade one to lay down life for an ideal, that knowledge within me that there is no fulfilment but in giving. Is that what I am trying to do? I came to the conclusion that on this earth there is only one value, one reality, life. I realised that somehow I must try to be great enough in spirit to help others show love to the whole world, like those who have shown me love here. Then I remembered what Lyn Harris had told us, that we must not be warped to the purposes of leaders who would have us hate each other blindly, and that we must each try to remain unswayed by the shouts of the crowd, and that we must keep our ideals quietly and try to share them with others. I know everyone has to make up their own views, but at the moment I know these to be mine.

It says much for the democratic and tolerant society in Britain that, at a desperate time of total war and survival, allowance could still be made for conscientious objectors. Without doubt we had a far easier time than conscientious objectors had had in the First World War, who had done so much to pioneer the way. Among the civilian population, through the shared traumas of war, a climate of openness and helpfulness had developed, which had brought a marvellous spirit of friendship towards each other. I wanted to be a part of this, but as a conscientious objector one inevitably felt removed from this fellowship. It was hard for an alive young person to realise that when Vera Lynn sang her wartime sentimental songs she was not singing for me. Certainly, I later found it more comfortable to be in an overseas section of the FAU, involved in needy work, and sharing just a little the hardships and dangers of those in the Army. Somewhat to my surprise I found a mutual respect between the Army and the FAU: certainly we almost always had excellent relations and considerable understanding of our position from most of the officers of the British Army units we had dealings with. In a quiet way I think we made some witness, and, apart from the brief occurrence recorded in Chapter 8, I became more sure that what I was doing was the right thing for me. If one wanted to find better ways of resolving conflict then it had to start somewhere. However, there was always the awareness that, had the military situation gone differently, my witness would have been very much harder and I would probably have ended up in just such a camp as Sandbostel.

I have written more extensively about the FAU in general in an appendix at the end of this book, but it may be helpful to say here a little about the Relief Section, of which I was a part. Every member of the FAU had had to pass through a training camp. There were some twenty during the war. In the beginning the average age in these camps was nearer twenty than thirty. Roughly half were members of the Society of Friends or had been educated at Friends' schools. The FAU relief teams in Europe generally reflected this balance. However, in this respect 2 FAU was unusual; at the time of the events described in this book, four members were in their thirties, five in their twenties and four still in their nineteenth year. Of the thirteen members only Roger Stanger and myself came from a Quaker background, but all had a Christian affiliation.

We came from a variety of experience. Len Darling, the Section Leader, had been a professional footballer, captain of Brighton and Hove Football Club; after the war he became a schoolteacher. Dennis Wickham, the deputy leader, had been a librarian; George Champion, a civil servant; Arthur Jewson had worked in a bank, and Harry Gaunt in Cadbury's chocolate factory. Martin Southwood had left his studies at university, while David Curtis, Roger Stanger and myself had come straight from school. Gordon Taylor, the youngest member of the team, had been a clerk. I don't think I ever knew the backgrounds of Colin Sowerbutts, Hugh Johnes or John Freshwater.

In addition to certificate courses in First Aid and Home Nursing, the basic training camp included physical training, some catering and practical exercises in the field. All members then went on to have periods gaining practical experience in large hospitals. This included work on medical and surgical wards, outpatients and casualty, and a few had time in operating theatres. Most went on to learn to drive and to be taught basic vehicle mechanics and maintenance. All had been on a relief work and crash language course.

I had an interesting diversion while at Lewisham Hospital in London, where I had been sent for hospital experience. Towards the end of my training camp, at Manor Farm, Northfield, in Birmingham, we had a talk from Professor Kenneth Mellanby on malaria. As the war in the Far East spread the Japanese had gained control of 90 per cent of the world's production of Quinine, at the time the main drug used in the treatment of malaria. A virtually untried alternative had been found, Atebrin or

Mepacrine, and Professor Mellanby was engaged in experiments to discover whether it could be used as a prophylactic, and if so the most effective dosage. He was seeking volunteers to act as human guinea pigs in these experiments. We were young and keen to prove our readiness to help wherever we felt we could and many offered him their services in this way. I was one of a group of four or five at Lewisham Hospital who took different, monitored doses of Mepacrine, and were then bitten by mosquitoes carrying Benign Tertiary Malaria, a virulent strain. Although we all turned various shades of yellow, we had no other adverse side effects, and none succumbed to the disease. I heard later that some in other groups were not so lucky. We gained clinical experience by taking blood samples from ourselves and each other, which were used to discover the effectiveness of the drug. Mepacrine became widely used on a prophylactic basis with troops in the Far East. The story of these experiments is to be included in a history of human experimentation currently being written by Dr Jenny Hazelgrove of Nottingham University Medical School.[4]

During the air raids on London we would have to fire-watch on the hospital roof, to cope with any incendiary bombs, and then rush down to the outpatients department as the casualties were brought in from the surrounding district. Following my time at Lewisham I had experience in three other hospitals: Barnsley Hall in Bromsgrove, Ronkswood Hospital in Worcester and Bangour Hospital in Scotland, where I followed the usual pattern working in wards, casualty, theatres and even for a short time in an X-ray department. Later I learnt to drive and maintain vehicles at a course in Clent, Worcestershire, and finally did a relief work course in Birmingham, just prior to going to Europe.

Chapter 1

FAU Relief Teams In Northwest Europe[5]

The Friends Ambulance Unit was formed at the outbreak of the First World War in 1914 by a group of individual Quakers, but was administratively and financially independent of the Religious Society of Friends. It was laid down after the war in 1919. In 1939 a committee of First World War members re-established the FAU for men of military age who shared the Quaker view on war and peace, and had been conditionally registered as conscientious objectors. Later women were welcomed. The main focus was on work abroad, and as the war spread FAU teams could be found in many parts of the world. (See Appendix, p.120.)

In 1943 a number of British voluntary societies interested in overseas relief work who had been holding occasional meetings together, formed the Council of British Societies for Relief Abroad (COBSRA). Its purpose was to ensure co-ordination of effort, and to act as a channel through which societies could negotiate with the government for advancing their relief activities. Members of the FAU sat on its General Purposes Committee.

The Civil Affairs Branch of the British Army, and later the United Nations Relief and Rehabilitation Administration (UNRRA) had the responsibility for the government of liberated areas, including relief. It was, therefore, necessary for COBSRA to negotiate suitable agreements with them for the deployment of voluntary teams and the granting of the necessary facilities.

As the invasion of Europe approached, the FAU, with many of its members trained and immediately available, was well suited to act as the spearhead of the voluntary societies. Thus, following the Allied landings in France in June 1944, FAU Relief Sections Nos 1 and 2, of twelve men each, under the auspices of the British Red Cross, were put

Lunch break for some members of 2 FAU and 5 FAU in Belgium, January 1945

ashore with their eight vehicles from a tank landing craft on the beach at Arromanches in Normandy on the evening of 6 September, exactly three months after the D Day landings.

Although the armies had by then moved forward, there was still much immediate help required by civilians in the many destroyed villages in the aftermath of the savage fighting in Normandy. The two FAU Relief Sections were allocated to Detachments of the British Army's Civilian Affairs Branch (CAD), and good relations were soon established. The CADs provided the Relief teams with their means of existence and gave general direction to their work. Soon after arriving, however, 2 FAU, led by Len Darling, was called forward to Belgium to a refugee camp at Bourg Leopold which had just been liberated:

> Under the Section Leader's general supervision, individual members controlled the reception point to which Army transport brought refugees, the registration room in which personal details were recorded, the disinfecting room where DDT anti-louse powder was sprayed up the sleeves, down the neck and trouser legs, the departure enclosure from which Army lorries took the refugees to camps away from the front, and also camp stores. Later catering and sleeping arrangements were added to this list. Ambulances were manned whenever they were needed.[6]

This pattern of working, which became known as 'the chain', was followed from then on wherever the section ran camps, although modifications were sometimes needed to meet differing circumstances. Later 2 FAU did similar work in the Netherlands, and co-operated with Dutch civilian medical authorities in Nijmegen during the airborne forces battle at Arnhem, often under artillery fire.

'Early in November 1944 the Civil Affairs Director of 21st Army Group, having received reports from his Corps H.Q.s on the work of the two FAU Sections in Holland, made direct approach to Gerald Gardiner [overall leader of the two FAU teams], for five more Sections, in order to provide each Army Corps in the Group with similar assistance.'[7] Subsequently, Gerald Gardiner brought over 55 members with vehicles on the 31 December 1944. I was with this party. There was a general transfer of personnel between the now seven sections, so that each team had a balance of experienced individuals.

Gerald Gardiner was not a typical member of the FAU. As a barrister and well into his fifties he was not subject to call-up for military service, and able to follow his profession. However, he had long decided that if he was called up he would register as a conscientious objector. With his pacifist belief he came to feel that continuing in his job didn't seem right, and he applied to join the FAU. He was accepted and was probably the only member of the FAU who was over call-up age and had not gone through the tribunal system. In later life he was appointed Lord Chancellor during the government of Harold Wilson in 1964. During his six years in office capital punishment was abolished, and laws regarding abortion and homosexuality were reformed. He appointed the first women judge to the High Court and introduced a compulsory training programme for Justices of the Peace.

The reconstituted 2 FAU which I had now joined, then followed the fighting as it advanced in Belgium, the Netherlands and Germany. It ran emergency camps for refugees and displaced persons in the Ardennes as the British Army repelled the final major German advance of the war, and then again following the battle in the Reichswald as the British Army entered Germany. On 15 February 1945 2 FAU moved to a spacious colony for the care of the mentally ill and epileptics, at Bedburg, near Cleves, in Germany at 2.30 pm on the day of its capture. Len Darling wrote:

> The place was chaotic when we arrived; troops occupying buildings, in the cellars of which were sheltering some 3000 refugees. German troops were only three hundred yards away and the civilians had planted themselves in the numerous cellars during the fighting overhead. Of the establishment itself there remained some 1000 mental patients, 300 staff and 800 staff families. No light was functioning and water for half an hour a day only; the refugees had been existing on whatever small stocks they had first taken to ground with them. Fighting going on overhead restricted their movement and when we came the situation was one glorious hotchpotch of disorder. To add to this, new refugees started coming in on our first day here, amongst whom were several hundreds of Displaced Persons. We could only start coping with the new arrivals, who, in the first three days numbered some 3000.[8]

On 25 February – I realised only some days later that my twentieth birthday on the 18th had passed unnoticed – I wrote home to my parents:

Transporting DPs away from the fighting in the Rhineland from an assembly point and camp run by 2 FAU, near Goch, March 1945

We moved some ten days ago and have been extremely busy ever since. The journey here was through devastated country and blighted forest [Reichswald]. The roads were very muddy and shell cratered, in places felled tree trunks had been placed so that vehicles could drive over the holes. Firing was going on and there was much evidence of recent tank battles. Several tanks were still smouldering. We arrived in this little 'town' [Bedburg] five hours after its capture, and troops were still 'mopping up'. The place is very badly damaged and a haze of dust still hangs in the air. We found some billets in a not too damaged house, and spent a disturbed night 300 yards from German troops, within the sound of mortar and gun fire. Next day we worked with British artillery firing over our heads into the German positions from time to time. There was a great deal to do. In the cellars of dozens of blitzed buildings were thousands of refugees, many with untreated wounds. They have been underground for four days and nights, packed like sardines, in dreadful squalor. Children without mothers and mothers looking for lost children. More refugees come in hourly. No food or water and little undamaged housing. We were visited by the Luftwaffe [German Air Force] on one occasion when a group of us were surveying a building for a temporary hospital and bombs were dropped. Fortunately the building we were in was not hit but doors and windows came in and we were all flung across the room. David [Curtis] received a slightly cut face from flying glass, but miraculously the rest of us were quite unharmed, although shaken. The 'settlement', rather than a town, quickly became known and was visited by numerous war correspondents. Among them was old Buckley, but he didn't really remember me. His report on the visit appeared in the *Daily Telegraph* for 22nd February. We also had a BBC recording van and Gaumont British News, who briefly filmed some of our chaps. I would like to tell you more of what we are doing in this extraordinary place, but apparently security doesn't allow us.

Christopher Buckley had been a Classical history teacher at my school (St Christopher School, Letchworth) before the war. He became a well-known frontline war correspondent, but was later tragically killed by a landmine explosion during the Korean War.

With the entry into Germany the British CAD to which the FAU teams were attached, had been renamed Military Government Detachments

(Mil Gov Det). The War Diary of 205, Mil Gov Det,[9] recorded that on 19 February a refugee girl was killed and her mother injured by mortar fire in front of the registration building. Registration was then moved further back to another building for greater safety. The War Diary also records that on the 21st the colony was dive-bombed; another refugee girl was killed and the building housing the medical supplies was badly damaged. The isolation hospital was also hit and all the patients had to be evacuated. On the 23rd the colony was visited by Field Marshal Montgomery, commander in chief of all the British forces, but I have no recollection of this event. The administration of the colony was handed over to 605 Mil Gov Det on 28 February, when there were some seven thousand refugees and DPs.

I wrote home again on 28 February:

> At last some life is coming back to this place. It took twelve days before the birds started singing again. It makes you realise how wonderful nature is. Even on trees which have had branches blasted off, little buds are showing and regaining life. Now all is much quieter but we are still very busy, although not so urgently. Refugees continue to come in, mostly in a pretty poor state. As an example; of twenty extended families, about 120 people, fifteen were incomplete, that is with some member dead or missing, and every family had an injured or sick member amongst them. We are shortly handing over our work here to Richard Wainwright's FAU Section 5, so I expect we will be moving forward again.

Richard Wainwright later became Gerald Gardiner's deputy. After the war he became known as Liberal MP for Colne Valley, and Party spokesman on financial matters.

The colony at Bedburg became a Refugee Centre extended by a great many tents, and eventually housed over twenty-five thousand people. An FAU team remained there, the only element of continuity, until virtually all the German civilians had been dispersed again at the end of April. After the Rhine was crossed, the care of displaced persons (DPs) became the main task of the FAU Relief Sections:

> Within a fortnight of the crossing all the Sections were hastily organising camps for former forced labourers, and also escaped prisoners of war of twenty or more different nationalities. Some groups had assembled in camps of their own choosing, often the communal living quarters which had been their homes during the period of forced labour. In other cases, they were roaming the countryside and living on plunder, and only moving into official camps under pressure of hunger, bad weather, or rumours of homeward transport and direction by military patrols. The Relief Sections had to move on every few days, as soon as basic needs had been met in each new centre which could then be handed over to some other Military Government formation or UNRRA.[10]

In a few short months 2 FAU had gained considerable experience of the work: arranging sleeping accommodation, feeding and foraging for food, finding wood for cooking and heating water, sanitation, water supply, registration, medical examination and treatment, delousing, dealing with language problems, organising parties of DPs to carry out much of this work, transportation to hospital, and so on. Many thousands had passed through their camps since the team had left France. So much of the work of the FAU Relief Sections at this time had had to be of a 'First Aid' nature, emergency improvisation. Not until the fighting ceased did this gradually change to longer-term measures.[11]

From 14 to 29 April 2 FAU, attached to 205 Mil Gov Det, a part of 30 Corps, were located at the village of Holtzhausen, near the town of Harpstedt, south of Bremen. We were running a large tented camp for DPs of many nationalities. Western nationals were on their way home,

2 FAU convoy arriving at Harpstedt, April 1945. Bremen still in German hands. The soldier on bicycle to right of picture had come to warn us not to turn left as the road ran straight in to the German positions! From left to right, Arthur Jewson, Hugh Johnes and Dennis Wickham

their stay was quite short as rail transport of some sort westwards had been rapidly re-established. Because of the fighting there was no eastbound traffic. So Russians, Poles, Czechs, Yugoslavs and others had to be housed and fed until the German Army surrendered. In some cases there were camps for these people for several years, and some never did wish to return to their home countries, now occupied by Russia, and became absorbed into the local population. It was here on 29 April that we had news of the concentration camp at Sandbostel.

It seems appropriate to conclude this chapter with the following acknowledgement. General Sir Miles Dempsey, Commander of the 2nd Army, wrote at the end of hostilities to the Director of Military Government 21 Army Group:

Setting up our tented accommodation in a field off the Harpstedt to Bassum road, April 1945. From left to right, Gordon Taylor, Colin Sowerbutts, Arthur Jewson, Hugh Johnes, Len Darling and John Freshwater

Dealing with an 'officious' Colin Sowerbutts while setting up camp, April 1945. From left to right, Arthur Jewson, Hugh Johnes and Len Darling

I would be grateful if you would convey to the appropriate authorities my grateful thanks for the splendid work of the FAU teams with 2nd Army. Not only have they been invaluable, they also had the great merit of being available when they were needed. They have filled a gap in our organisation with the greatest cheerfulness and efficiency. No hardship has been too great and no work too hard for them. They have fitted in admirably to our relief organisation. If we had to repeat the Normandy landing I would ask for more and land them earlier. In particular I give high praise to the FAU teams who have been with us since the bridgehead days with Corps Refugee Detachments. What they do not know about handling refugees is not worth knowing.

CHAPTER 2

Sandbostel

The British Army had long been aware that there was a prisoner-of-war camp at Sandbostel, Stalag XB. But it was not known that in a separate compound there were several thousand 'political' prisoners whose plight was desperate. This distressing news was brought by two PoWs, an Englishman and a Frenchman, who managed to escape the Camp and make their way to the British lines on 28 April. (See Chapter 5.)

In view of this information the British Army decided to free its inmates immediately. The British troops who had just captured Bremen, 30 Corps, who were pressing forward to clear the area between the Weser and Elbe rivers, were delegated to do this. 2 FAU was attached to 205 Mil Gov Det, which was a part of 30 Corps. Application was made to the German forces facing 30 Corps for permission to enter the Camp, but, as this was refused, the Guards Armoured Division turned aside to make an assault crossing of the river Oste, and on the evening of 29 April overran the Camp. On the morning of 30 April senior Army medical officers visited the Camp and it was decided that the medical services of 30 Corps should do everything possible to provide the medical attention that was so desperately needed, compatible with their responsibilities to the formations still heavily involved in the fighting. 168 Light Field Ambulance and 31 Field Hygiene Section were moved to the Camp the next day.[12]

I am indebted to *The Medical History of the Second World War* edited by F.A.E Crew for this information, but a more detailed and personal account has been given by Captain Robert Barer, an RAMC doctor, who was the first British officer to enter the Camp. In a report on Sandbostel he wrote:

We first heard reports of Sandbostel two weeks before its capture. A patrol of the Household Cavalry had got quite near the Camp and had caused some confusion among the Camp guards who thought our main body was coming. A number of British Secret Service men had escaped a few days later and they gave us very useful and accurate information about conditions in the Camp. [It is not clear whether the men referred to here were the same as the prisoners of war mentioned by Crew or others, and if so which were the first to escape. Captain Barer's report was written shortly after the events, but Crew's book was compiled some years later when, presumably, more information had become available.] Recently, however, the SS had brought in about 8000 political prisoners from other concentration camps, and despite the horrified protests of the German Commandant, had dumped them in a corner of the Camp. The SS allowed no one to enter the political prisoners' compound. They even refused the German Camp Doctor permission to enter. It was obvious that conditions in the compound were very bad.

With the approach of the British forces:

> The SS packed up and went. The German Camp Commandant and his staff remained, but handed over the administration of the Camp to Colonel Albert, a French prisoner of war. A French Naval Medical Officer, and the German camp doctor were able to enter the political compound and at great risk had removed a number of typhus cases to a separate hospital hut. This was an important piece of news. It confirmed the presence of typhus, though we had no idea of its extent. It meant that extreme care would have to be taken in capturing the Camp to ensure that none of our troops contracted the disease. Plans were made accordingly. Orders were issued that no troops were to enter the Camp itself until a medical officer had reported on the typhus situation. All troops were to be dusted with anti-louse powder and if possible inoculated. No prisoners were to be allowed to leave the Camp as there was a grave danger that disease might get spread about the countryside and among our troops.

It is perhaps necessary to explain that Epidemic Typhus is spread between humans by body lice, and without treatment is usually terminal. In the crowded and insanitary conditions at Sandbostel, delousing with anti-louse powder (DDT) became a vital exercise.

Captain Barer joined a long column of vehicles bearing a PoW contact team composed of officers of every nationality, who were to enter the Camp as soon as he had reported on the typhus situation. He describes in detail the very difficult attack on the German forces surrounding the Camp and his personal involvement in it. After a day and a night he finally entered the PoW camp and got to the Camp hospital:

> Here we got a tremendous reception. There were 2000 patients and 40 doctors of all nationalities. I was introduced to all the doctors and had to salute and shake hands with each one individually. At last I managed to take a pencil in my aching hand and made a few notes. The hospital (only for the prisoners of war) appeared to be well equipped and well run. I made a note of certain medical requirements and after a final salute all round I made my escape, still flushed with embarrassment.

As the enemy were cleared he was able to enter further into the Camp through masses of cheering PoWs. He met the French Commandant and the French Naval Officer in charge of the typhus ward. There were 122 cases in the ward, but a quite unknown number still in the political prisoners' compound:

> We approached the political prisoners' compound and saw the gate was marked with the skull and crossbones, with the word 'Typhus' underneath. Suddenly I was panic stricken as I had left the tin of antilouse powder in the Jeep. However it was too late to do anything so I kept quiet. The first thing I noticed in the compound was the smell, which got stronger as we approached the huts. I cannot attempt to describe it, but I never got rid of that smell from my nostrils for several days. Outside the huts odd groups of men were standing or lying.

Captain Barer goes on to describe in graphic detail how he went through the whole compound, entering hut after hut, through dark passages, over floorboards rotted through and slimy with filth, stumbling over bodies, mostly dead. During the night the Royal Engineers completed building a bridge over the river and in the morning he was able to bring up his Field Ambulance and Hygiene sections to set about delousing. The following morning he handed over his commitments to them and left the camp. I make further references to this remarkable man in a later chapter.[13]

The Camp was situated on a stretch of bare and bleak heathland, with a small road running past the gate. It was comprised of many large and smaller wooden barrack-like buildings, surrounded by tall barbed-wire fences, with watchtowers on the perimeters. It divided into three different sections. The first and second accommodated some fifteen thousand PoWs. The first was occupied mainly by Western nationals, mostly French, British and Canadians. Conditions were not good but as far as we could tell they had been treated within the terms of the International Red Cross Convention, although many of those in the Camp hospital were in a poorly condition. Those in the second section, mainly for Russian PoWs, without the protection of the Convention, were much worse. They had been fed less food than the Westerners. But even here the conditions could not compare with those in the third section, a concentration camp for some eight thousand civilian 'political' prisoners.

Hugh Johnes, a member of 2 FAU, was to write, 'I shall never be able to eradicate from my memory the scenes and the stench. Behind barbed

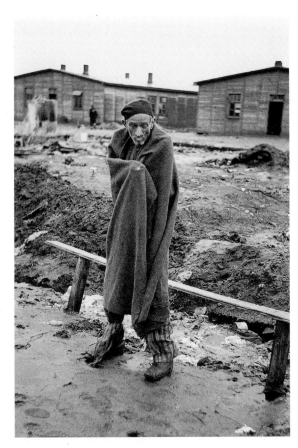

InsideSandbostel concentration camp. Political prisoner, a Hungarian Jew, one of those who were still able to stand. 30 April. Photo: Imperial War Museum

wire, thrusting their hands through in pleas for food were human skeletons, skin and bone, dressed or half dressed, some with tops and some with bottoms, none it seemed with whole outfits, in pyjama-like striped filthy rags. They dribbled their incomprehensibly mouthed appeals for food.'[14]

Bodies strewn all over the Camp, where they had died on the spot. The scene that confronted the rescuers on 1 May. Photos: Imperial War Museum

The official Army medical history recorded:

> The PoW portion of the camp was overcrowded but otherwise fairly satisfactory. In its hospital there were 1840 patients whose condition was likewise fairly satisfactory. But in the compound occupied by the political prisoners the conditions were utterly horrifying. In hutted accommodation, adequate maybe for about 2000, were between 7000 and 8000 emaciated males of fifteen years and upwards. The great majority of them were in a deplorable state of malnutrition. Starved and gravely ill men in filthy rags lay huddled on the bare floor boards. Everywhere the dead and dying sprawled amid the slime of human excrement. To 168 Light Field Ambulance and 31 Field Hygiene Section was assigned the herculean task of coping with the problems that these conditions presented. There were no interior sanitary arrangements, and even if there had been, large numbers of the prisoners were far too weak and far too apathetic to have made use of them. Diarrhoea was universal and so everywhere inside and outside the huts was grossly polluted. There was no food and apparently no facilities for providing it. [Other accounts vary on this point, and there was certainly a large kitchen.] It was learned that periodically a cartload of raw turnips had been thrown into the compound to be seized by those as were still able to compete. For water the prisoners had depended on a large stagnant pool in the compound and this had inevitably become grossly contaminated and evil-smelling.[15]

As recorded earlier, 2 FAU were occupied in running a large camp for displaced persons near Harpstedt from 14 to 29 April. It was here on the 29th that we had news of the concentration camp at Sandbostel, and the British Army's decision to liberate it immediately.

Len Darling, the team's leader, hurriedly called a meeting of all 2 FAU members, and it was agreed that we should accompany 205 Mil Gov Det and offer what help we could. Len, having been briefed by Mil Gov, advised on the exercise before us. The object was to move quickly so as to save as many lives as possible. Units of the Army were to care for the PoWs and arrange for their return home, secure the German guard, provide food, organise the burial of the dead and finally destroy the Camp. We understood that an RAMC unit, 168 Light Field Ambulance, were moving to the Camp to take charge of the medical side, and their doctors would be available to advise on the feeding. The FAU team were to take charge of the kitchen and feeding, help supervise the teams of local civilians being brought in to help in clearing up the Camp, to help with the care of the rescued inmates, and to assist wherever there was need. The tents and equipment of the present DP camp were to be left in place for another team to take over. Further equipment and more army personnel were arriving and a large convoy was being assembled in a very short time.

It had been decided by higher authority that, as Germans had created this horror camp, they should help clear it up. Some sixty to seventy young German women, including many high school girls, were made to report by the British Army, through the local police, in the centre of Delmenhorst, a small town west of Bremen. Army trucks transporting the women joined the convoy which was gathering at the DP camp at

Harpstedt. The women were always well-fed and in most cases had small bundles of belongings with them. They had been given no information and did not know where they were going. Some even feared it might be a form of revenge and that they were destined for a sex camp. The FAU team were not very happy with this development, but recognised that there was little time if lives were to be saved and all the help that could be raised was going to be needed.

Despite the Army's strict non-fraternisation rule, one or two members of the FAU team were able to make contact with the women and give some assurance as to their safety. Later we discovered that similar groups of women had been collected from other areas and taken to the Camp. The stories of a few of these women are told in Chapter 6. In the event the help of these women proved crucial to the saving of many lives.

Trucks and ambulances were rapidly loaded, and the FAU/Mil Gov convoy moved off on the afternoon of 30 April. Once the suburbs of Bremen were passed, progress was slow. The conditions of the roads were appalling: bombing had left huge craters which had been roughly filled with rubble, bridges had been blown up and only in some places had the Army replaced them with temporary Bailey bridges. In one part the autobahn (motorway) had been lifted to a crazy angle, and steady driving was called for. It became difficult to read maps in the growing darkness. The sound of gunfire and artillery flashes lit up the night sky. Headlights were masked to very thin slits of light and it was necessary to keep a very watchful eye on the white-painted differential axle of the vehicle in front. I am grateful to Gordon Taylor, a member of the FAU team, for much of the information about this journey which he recorded soon after the events in his unpublished memoirs.

Dennis Wickham wrote in his diary on 30 April:
> Loaded Section stores in the morning. Moved off about 2.30 pm. We are taking 12 Polish DPs from the camp in our vehicles to help us. Another long wait to get over the Weser Bridge. [All the bridges over the river Weser had been blown up or bombed and this was the only one, a temporary single lane pontoon bridge built by the Royal Engineers and coping with all the Army traffic in both directions.] Got on to autobahn running from Bremen to Hamburg. These autobahns are straight, dual carriageways, concrete roads. There are no crossroads, but intersecting routes are carried overhead, giving a very fine effect. The country around is comprised of huge tracts of arable land and some heath. We went some 40 or 50 miles too far along this road almost to Hamburg, where fighting is still taking place. Most of the night was spent trying to find the correct route, finally we gave up the quest.

The convoy came to a halt near a heavily wooded area, and everyone disembarked to stretch cramped limbs. It appeared we were lost. Packages of food were passed round. Cigarettes glowed in the darkness. No vehicle passed us in either direction the whole day or night. Up ahead distant gunfire could still be heard. The German women went into the woods; some may not have returned, but no one seemed to mind. They were probably safer with us than in open country with all the released DPs roaming about. The rest of the night was spent uncomfortably and frozen stiff in the open cabs of our trucks and ambulances, trying to get some sleep and wondering what was in store for us.

The morning came early. In order to keep us warm, fires were lit on the grass partition between the carriageways, and from somewhere came hot sweet tea and more sandwiches. During the night our location had been established and contact made with the advancing British troops ahead. The convoy moved off again, and finally arrived at Sandbostel during the day of 1 May. That evening Dennis wrote in his diary, 'Reached Sandbostel late in the afternoon, the last hours being over a simply appalling road. As a matter of fact an REME recovery vehicle accompanied the convoy as a precaution. The FAU Leyland six-tonner had to tow one of our Austin ambulances as Roger had driven straight into its rear, smashing in the front and radiator.'

In a field, opposite the Camp's forbidding gate, tents for sleeping and eating were erected and other requirements for camp life established. We awaited the reports of the Army medical staff who had been making initial investigations in the Camp. Also on 1 May Dennis wrote:

> Went over the Camp this evening. It is just horrible. PoW section wasn't too bad, though some of these fellows looked ill. But when we came to the civilian compound no words can adequately describe the scenes of horror. Typhus, typhoid and TB were throughout the Camp. People were dying at the rate of 150 a day [several differing estimates have been recorded]. Large pits were filled with corpses. Bodies piled in mounds about the yards. Others

lying virtually naked in rooms, grotesque figures, crouching in corners too weak to move, awaiting their turn to die. The stench was horrible, no sanitation whatsoever. Rooms far worse than any pigsty. The living merely skeletons, little or no clothes, just skin and bones and ashen grey colouring. I would never have believed such a thing possible. What is more, cannibalism is present. It sounds fantastic, but it is true. There are several watchtowers and guards at the gate. A crowd of PoWs had collected at the gate watching the guards fire at some inmates running across the bare moor trying to escape. Anyone who does get away is a potential carrier of typhus and disease. It is a large camp consisting of long single-storied hutments and surrounded with barbed wire with observation posts equipped with searchlights at every corner. In the Stalag PoW camp I met two British prisoners. They were fortunate as they had only been captured six weeks before. The German troops are still only a mile or so away.

CHAPTER 3

The Rescue Operation

Early the following morning the concentration camp was entered and the dreadful work started. A quite overwhelming task confronted the small contingent of RAMC and other Army personel, the FAU team, and the German helpers. A fearful smell, impossible to describe, drifted everywhere. A huge pit had been dug by the Germans in the centre of the compound before they had left, into which row upon row of half clothed and naked bodies had been thrown and lime scattered over them.

There were some eight thousand political prisoners, all male, dying in large numbers every day. At the gate of the Camp the rescuing personnel entered walking through a powder substance, and gloves, masks and overalls were issued. The German women helped to carry the dead bodies, more every hour, for placing in the pits. Two smaller ones had to be dug by the Army using a mechanical digger. Those inmates showing signs of life were transported to another compound outside the perimeter of the concentration camp, where six huts which had been occupied by the German guards were selected by 168 Lt Fd Amb for conversion to an improvised hospital. These huts were rapidly cleansed on 1 May, and the first 287 patients requiring immediate hospitalisation were moved in the next day.

> They were first passed through a 'human laundry', a large marquee, in the PoW camp close to the political prisoners' compound, with twenty tables. The patient from the compound was brought in at the 'dirty' end, his clothing, such as it was, removed and all hair-bearing areas shaved. He was then carried to one of the tables and washed thoroughly with soap and water. Then he was dried and dusted with DDT, wrapped in a clean blanket, placed on a stretcher and transported to the improvised hospital about half a mile away. From May 1st to May 6th, some 300 patients each day were thus transferred.[16]

168 Lt Fd Amb, whose participation was so crucial to the whole operation in the early days, consisted of just ten officers (one not a doctor) and 112 other ranks. They were reinforced, according to their War Diary,[17] by two German military doctors, six civilian doctors, 66 German nurses, and 185 German civilian women, some of these living on the campsite and others reporting daily, under Mil Gov arrangements.

The War Diary of 205 Mil Gov Det[18] recorded on 1 May that the Detachment's responsibilities had been defined as the provision of as much foodstuffs from local resources as possible, for the use of the whole camp, including the PoWs, and the procurement of stores, equipment and clothing as necessary. The Detachment was also fully responsible for the administration of that part of the Camp occupied by the political prisoners and known as 'Horror' Camps 1 and 2. The War Diary said, 'Sandbostel is a one-third replica of Belsen and to clear up seems an impossible task. Hundreds of corpses buried today. German labour, male and female, impressed to carry out this and other unpleasant duties.' It continued:

> 168 Lt Fd Amb have now organised a 'human laundry' modelled on that at Belsen and are doing a marvellous job of work, evacuating probable survivors to an improvised hospital just outside the Camp. 205 inspired by the efforts of 168 and assisted by other Mil Gov Dets in the area are procuring tons of foodstuffs, equipment and stores from the locality. Deaths are now approximately 100 a day, many through typhus, and not a hope of ascertaining who they were or where they came from. German impressed labour, about 400, kept busy removing and burying corpses. (3 May)

> 'Human laundry' processing 600 a day [Crew says 300 a day]. Deaths are occurring during the process. Survivors most of whom are unable to speak, express their gratitude and the job now not only seems possible but so well worth doing. All concerned are working at utmost pressure and after the day's work conferences commence, continuing until well after midnight. (4 May)

The FAU team was asked by Mil Gov to be responsible for organising the feeding arrangements of those in the compound, and Martin

Southwood, who had had some catering training, was put in charge of the kitchen. This had been the task of a French Lieutenant. French PoWs had taken control of the Camp when most of the SS and German Army guards had departed some ten days before the arrival of the British Army. Under these arrangements the inmates had received ersatz coffee with a little milk in the morning and three-quarters of a litre of very watery soup in the afternoon, sometimes a little bread and a minute quantity of margarine when possible. But the French could do little but await the arrival of the British Army. M.C. Carey, editor of the British Red Cross journal, *Over to You*, wrote in the August 1945 issue, 'The evening the FAU Relief Section started work each internee received two eggs, biscuits and cheese, some tinned meat or fish and ten cigarettes. From that moment contentment began to spread, and morale to rise.'

Sadly, this observation was very optimistic, and the ration distribution described must have been for those who were somewhat better off, for there were very many too ill to feed themselves or able to digest even this light diet. It was not in accordance with the diet scales given us the next day by the doctors of 168 Lt Fd Amb. These were as follows:

'A' Two-hourly feeds for starved internees

Skimmed fresh milk	2	litres
or Dried skimmed milk	3	oz
Sugar	1	oz
Salt	$\frac{1}{2}$	oz
Compound Vitamin tablets	3	

'B' Normal hospital diet

Skimmed fresh milk	$1\frac{1}{2}$	litres
or Dried skimmed milk	3	oz
Sugar'	1	oz
Salt	$\frac{1}{4}$	oz
Compound Vitamin tablets	3	
Bread	5	oz
Potatoes	2	oz
Margarine/Butter	1	oz
Concentrated soup	$\frac{1}{2}$	oz
Tinned meat	1	oz
Tinned vegetables	2	oz

'C' Diet for those not in hospital

Dried milk	2	oz
Sugar	1	oz
Salt	$\frac{1}{2}$	oz
Compound Vitamin tablets	2	
Bread	6	oz
Potatoes	16	oz
Flour	2	oz
Concentrated soup	$\frac{1}{2}$	oz
Tinned meat	2	oz
Tinned vegetables	4	oz
or dehydrated vegetables	$\frac{1}{2}$	oz

The 'C' diet was prepared and distributed from the FAU kitchen in the compound, 'A' and 'B' from the kitchen in the improvised hospital. In the hospital those suffering from extreme dehydration, those unable to take fluids by the mouth because of weakness or apathy and typhus cases who were comatose were transfused. Plasma and 5 per cent glucose were given intravenously: 367 patients were treated in this way.[19]

The War Diary of 168 Lt Fd Amb gives a great deal of information on the treatment of the inmates, but makes no mention of the kitchen or feeding arrangements, perhaps because they were not directly involved, except to record the arrival on 5 May of four Army Catering Corps cooks lent by 8th Armoured Brigade. These must be 'the corporal and three privates of the Army Catering Corps' who according to Crew did all the food preparation, aided by some half-dozen French cooks from among the ex-PoWs.[20] Neither source makes mention of the FAU. It is possible that the blue-lettered 'Friends Ambulance Unit' shoulder flash on the khaki uniform could have been mistaken for 'French' during such a chaotic time. However, M.C. Carey, editor of the British Red Cross journal, *Over to You,* who visited the Camp in the early days, was not under any such misapprehension, as he recorded in an article in the August issue. I have no recollection of any Army cooks but I can still see Martin Southwood and others in those first four or five desperate days valiantly supervising the Camp kitchen with the help of several German women and French ex-PoWs. With the arrival of the Army cooks Martin may well have earned a well-deserved rest from his arduous duties. While researching for this book I tried unsuccessfully to trace Martin: his knowledge of the feeding arrangements would have been invaluable.

With the arrival of a larger unit, 10 Casualty Clearing Station, on 6 May, Crew writes, 'The kitchen thus far used by 168 Lt Fd Amb became the hospital kitchen with the CCS Sergeant Cook in charge. A staff kitchen was established in a garage building and staffed by Army Catering cooks to serve the German doctors and nurses and the resident female workers. A Company kitchen was established to serve the personnel of 10 CCS, the ex-internee doctors and the German PoW helpers.'[21] The FAU team ate with the officers of 205 Mil Gov Det in their tented mess.

Political prisoners carrying in tubs of soup to their less fortunate comrades who were unable to walk, 30 April. Photo: Imperial War Museum

The provision of food for these numbers became a vast undertaking coming from both Army supplies and local German sources. Crew writes, 'Later the Quarter Master made contact with the nearest DID [Detailed Issue Depot] of the Army to arrange for the daily supply of milk, eggs and bread. Mil Gov quickly succeeded in making available everything that was asked for.'[22] In the PoW camp a store of Red Cross food parcels was uncovered. It was decided to use these to help feed the inmates of the political compound. The Western PoWs would not need them as they were rapidly being transported home and most of the Eastern PoWs were being transferred to other camps. The parcels were passed to the FAU for use in the kitchen. I can remember Gordon and myself endlessly unpacking and sorting small tins and packets intended for individuals into like categories to help with the mass feeding.

Some understanding of the size of the operation in obtaining foodstuffs may be seen from the following figures recorded in 205 Mil Gov Det's War Diary: 'Taken into the Camp between 1–25 May. Milk 150,000 litres, eggs 245,000, butter 60,000 lbs, cheese 2000 lbs, herring 20 tons, beef 200,000 lbs, sugar 5 tons.'

Once the outside areas had been cleared, the huts were entered. Hugh Johnes wrote, 'the scenes were ghastly to behold; huts deep in filth and excreta, gaping holes in the roofs, windows in tatters'.[23] Mostly the men were lying in tiered bunks, many without blankets, but some just lay on the wooden boards of the floor. It was dark, the smell unbearable and the doctors had to face the terrible task of deciding between the living and the dead, and those who had a chance of survival and those who simply had to be left. Amazingly there were still some who could stand and walk a little.

The War Diary of 168 Lt Fd Amb records that on 2 May a further four barracks rooms were cleaned out and improvised as a new typhus hospital, as more cases were being found than had at first been anticipated. The first sixty cases were moved in on the same day. For 2 May Dennis wrote in his diary: 'Recced [reconnoitred] the typhus hospital today. We have

German women carrying typhus case to waiting ambulance en route to the hospital, 3 May. Photo: Imperial War Museum

transported some of the patients to a clean block. The old will be burned. Looked over the Camp kitchen. It was unbelievably filthy. I am responsible with Martin [Southwood] and Colin [Sowerbutts] for improvising kitchen and accommodation. Have been talking with the French Lieutenant [ex-PoW] who had been in charge of the kitchen.'

Some members of the FAU team were supervising groups of German women working in the 'human laundry' and with the feeding. On 3 May Dennis wrote:

Occupied this morning in ascertaining how many people in each block were in need of special diet owing to their starved condition, or should I say, their more hopeless condition compared with the starved condition of the average inmate. For this purpose I contacted two doctors one in the dirty camp, where there was definitely typhus and typhoid, and one in the 'clean' camp, that is where conditions are slightly, but only slightly, better. Some nine hundred inmates needed the special diet. The kitchen is being cleaned up slowly, new boilers are being installed. German men and women are being used to bury the dead, clean up the filth and destroy infested clothing. The Lt Fd Amb which is dealing with the hospitalisation of inmates has been doing an excellent job. Everyone in the Camp is slowly being washed and deloused, and the very sick transported between blankets to the improvised hospital. Those who are too far gone are being left to die. The stench everywhere is nauseating and lingers persistently in the nostrils. Two German jet planes were overhead today causing a lot of nuisance and there was some shelling yesterday.[24]

On 3 May I wrote home:

> we received an urgent movement order at our last DP camp and
> pulled out the following afternoon. We had a long way to go and
> spent a night on the Bremen–Hamburg autobahn, as travelling
> was very slow. We were advised that our job was to help clear up
> a PoW and concentration camp still in German hands. Typhus
> and typhoid were believed to be present. A truce had been arranged
> with the German Army and we moved in as soon as British troops
> had secured the area. There were about fifteen thousand PoWs
> and eight thousand civilian 'political' prisoners. Among the PoWs
> were 350 British, Canadian and American soldiers, but the vast
> majority are Russians. They have not had too bad a time of it,
> although their living conditions are pretty unclean and food is in
> short supply. But the concentration camp was terrible, to put it
> simply. It was not an 'extermination' camp, but it is estimated
> that over a hundred are dying each day from starvation and disease.
> I won't describe the squalor except to say that the dead were in
> piles and hundreds in open pits. They had been virtually unfed
> for ten days. I tell you I would rather see a soldier who had been
> killed in battle than the living dead who crawled around that place.
> But I am sure you have read enough of these places in the
> newspapers, although it must be hard to believe. I can tell you
> that they exist. I have seen things I shall never forget. We have
> had plenty to do since we arrived, a whole RAMC unit is in charge
> helped by some 250 German people, with nurses and a few doctors
> among them. The population of the surrounding villages have
> been brought round to see the 'horror' as a form of 'education'.

The worst huts have finally been cleared today and we understand that two flame-throwing tanks will be brought in to burn them down. I hope nothing is left but a bit of scorched earth! Those who could be saved have been taken, wrapped in blankets, heads shaved, washed and DDT powdered, and put in bunks in cleaned barracks which are making do as an improvised hospital. Here they are having carefully worked out diets and vitamin tablets. The death rate is now less. They are mostly being looked after by German nurses and other women. Our main job is the cooking and feeding for Camp 2, those who are not in such a desperate plight and can walk a bit. They are fed mainly on specially prepared soups. Some of the British PoWs had been here for five years, a few since Dunkirk, and had many questions to ask us. They were immediately transported away and may well be home by now.

My comment about a truce was only partially correct, as I explain more fully in Chapter 5.

On 4 May Dennis recorded, 'The Camp and kitchen are now very much cleaner. Had the job today of collecting rations for the Camp, also transporting the German women to and from the kitchen. Tonight as I write this Very lights are going up all along the front and have just listened to the wireless, the first time for months, and the great news is announced that all resistance in north-west Germany ceases at 8 am tomorrow morning.' On 5 May he wrote, 'PoWs are now being evacuated at the rate of a thousand a day. Today many Russians have also gone. The danger arising from the looting of food and clothing is thereby reduced. The PoWs had been allowed out of the Camp. It was a common sight to see them returning at all times during the day laden with loot or even leading in cows, sheep and pigs.'

Meanwhile in the improvised hospital it became clear by 5 May that the task was far beyond the powers of one Light Field Ambulance unit, and, with the imminent cessation of hostilities, 30 Corps moved 10 Casualty Clearing Station in to take over the hospital, leaving 168 Lt Fd Amb to concentrate on looking after the political prisoners' compound and its remaining inmates.[25]

Crew records the improvised hospital as consisting of, six wooden huts each about 40 yards long with a central corridor and a number of small rooms on either side fitted with accommodation for about two hundred patients; five wooden huts of a different pattern which could accommodate about six hundred patients altogether; one hut, in the process of being evacuated by German civilian female workers, which could accommodate about two hundred patients.

This gave a total of some 2000 beds. There was no lighting system and the water supply was intermittent and unfit for drinking. There were washing and bathing facilities but the drains were blocked and the floors under water. The area around these huts was cluttered with litter and debris of all kinds and pockmarked with stagnant pools. In the huts there were already over 1500 patients, living skeletons, naked, suffering from acute and advanced disease as well as from starvation and famine diarrhoea. Typhus was rampant but segregation was impossible. [Some segregation was achieved later.] Each patient had a straw palliasse and two, or even three, blankets. Most were too weak to leave their beds and the staff could not possibly answer their insistent demands for water or bedpans. Everywhere in the huts and outside men crouched over some form of receptacle or over no receptacle at all in the stress of acute diarrhoea. They were apathetic and indifferent to everything save the urgency of hunger and of pain. Liberation meant nothing to them. They displayed no sense of modesty and no emotion save a fretful, clamorous impatience to satisfy the pangs of hunger. 10 CCS took over the hospital on May 6th, when the number of patients was 1713 and the number of vacant beds 211. Deaths in the hospital up to this time had numbered 137.[26]

Dennis Wickham's diary entries continued:

Have been drawing rations for the Camp during the last few days from DID. This afternoon I recced the position re cleansing, bathing and delousing of the inmates and found that some four hundred could now be processed in a day. It is proposed to transfer the political prisoners (those still left in the original compound) to fresh barracks as soon as the PoWs have left, and with this in mind I went over seven of the Russian barracks in Camp 1, that is the 'dirty' camp, to ascertain which to move into first. There are still a few corpses lying around. The camp was in a horrible state. Have read a report of a Colonel Evans on the subject of Sandbostel in which the work of the FAU is commended.[27] (6 May)

Had to take over from Captain Hagger [an officer of 205 Mil Gov Det] the cleanliness, sanitation and economy of Camps 1 and 2, and the seven huts which are being evacuated by the Russian PoWs. It will be a colossal job. Spent much of the day liaising with the Field Hygiene Section. Gerald Gardiner [overall leader of all the FAU Relief Teams in northwest Europe] arrived this afternoon. Much jollification in the other ranks tents last night, the eve of VE Day. There are to date 197 cases of typhus in the Camp. (7 May)

Crew continues the story in the improvised hospital:

At the end of the first day following the take-over [by 10 CCS on 6 May] during which 199 more patients were admitted, there was a feeling of utter despondency; the task seemed quite hopeless. But on the following day 30 Corps brought the good news that 86 British General Hospital was being moved to Rotenburg on May 11th and would be accepting patients from 10 CCS. The effect of this was dissipated, however, when it was found that another 2500 of the political prisoners would need to be taken in to the hospital. Typhus was rife among them and those who were ambulant at the time of the uncovering had now collapsed. By May 10th the hospital had 2777 patients and had to expect an intake of 300 a day during the next week. Deaths were averaging 300 a day. Tentage now filled all available space around the huts. In the hospital area much had been done. The huts were beginning to acquire a neatness. The arrival of pyjamas had an astonishing effect upon the patients, previously seemingly unaffected by the change in their fortune; they began to display an interest in their appearance; modesty and dignity began to find expression. The admired attributes of socialised man, compassion, consideration for others, co-operation and the like, disappear when the food intake falls below a certain minimum and stays there, but reappears quite quickly as the food intake is increased. With the pyjamas came hope to tinge the atmosphere of the wards and to affect profoundly all who breathed it. Since death was now no longer inevitable the continuance of living became a matter of individual interest and importance. And the weather was fine and warm.[28]

George Champion remembers that he and Arthur Jewson, members of the FAU team, were given the job with army personnel of seeking out fresh clothing for the patients. A barge was discovered on the river Elbe that contained a great deal of clothing. This was commandeered with the help of a Russian Army officer (the Elbe at this time was the dividing line between the British and Russian zones of occupation), and transported back to Sandbostel, for the less sick inmates to wear. Crew records:

> The officer commanding 10 CCS himself took on the gigantic task of obtaining most of the following equipment for the hospital from one source or another. Pyjamas, shirts and other bed wear 3000, pillows 3000, pillowcases 6000, sheets 3000, knives, forks and spoons 3000 of each, plates 4000, feeding cups 500, sputum mugs 500, washing bowls 200, air cushions 200, thermometers 60, also towels, soap, face cloths, toothbrushes, rubber aprons, nursing overalls, washing tubs, water jugs, primus stoves, civilian clothes, more blankets, straw, beds, stoves, containers, ladles, baking trays, mincing machines, tin openers, and other kitchen equipment.[29]

It is not clear whether these supplies were in addition to those procured by 205 Mil Gov Det but I rather think they were. Their War Diary records the equipment taken into the Camp between 1and 25 May:

Bedding
Beds 1400
Blankets 13,200
Sheets 1100
Pillowslips 350
Pillows 500
Mattresses 250
Palliasses 250
Towels 400
Two-tiered bunks 600

Clothing
Suits, complete 1500
Jackets 1300
Trousers 1300
Pants 4600
Vests 4800
Socks 6100
Overcoats 800
Pullovers 300
Gloves 400
Waistcoats 600
Shirts 6100
Handkerchiefs 600
Shoes 1400 pairs
Boots 1450 pairs
Hats 100
Braces 100
Night clothes 200

Miscellaneous
Cookers 17
Cutlery 2000
Chinaware 2300
Misc. containers 270
Bowls 16
Baths 20
Prepared timber 18 tons
Stoves 35
Duckboards 100
Bandages 1 cwt
Cotton wool 1 cwt
Matches 500,000 boxes
Bed chambers 180
Mincing machines 6
Brooms 100

CHAPTER 4

The End Of The War

As the war in Europe drew to a close, A. Tegla Davies, chairman of the Executive Committee of the Council of the Friends Ambulance Unit, sent a postscript to all units of the FAU everywhere. It read:

> The war in Europe may soon be over. An armistice will be the occasion not only for services of thanksgiving – and the pacifist will have as much cause for thanksgiving as anyone – but for victory celebrations and revelry on a grand scale.
>
> Such victory celebrations will take place publicly; they will also be held privately, probably in every hospital or other centre in which the FAU works. It will be easy to be carried along by mass enthusiasm. On behalf of the Executive and Advisory Committee, I need do no more than ask members to show discretion and not, at the last stage of the war, to give any impression of invalidating the stand which they have made since it began.
>
> I am not asking that Sections should not celebrate the end of five years of war. Many will wish to do so let it be in the right way and

for the right reasons. That is different from celebrating victory. Nor should we be lacking in understanding and give offence to those who, having for so long pursued the war with sincerity and devotion will find emotions unleashed which we cannot share.

We cannot share in celebrations of military victory. Let our prevailing mood be one of thanksgiving that the war is over and dedication to the cause of peace. And let our conduct fit our mood.

Dennis Wickham wrote on 8 May:

Listened to Mr Churchill's speech at 3 pm and the King's at 9 pm. In the evening went to an ENSA concert [we had been requested to attend by Major Sharp, Officer Commanding 205 Mil Gov Det], given in the open air at the back of our tents. Many bonfires lit all around to celebrate VE Day. At one minute past midnight tonight the unconditional surrender comes into force.

To celebrate the end of the fighting in Europe the Officer's Mess of 205 Mil Gov Det had a special evening meal to which the FAU and all the Detachment's other ranks were invited. Even wine was served. In the circumstances it was a splendid meal conjured up mostly from Army rations and prepared by the Detachment's Scottish Sergeant Cook, known to all as 'Jock'. Gordon Taylor recalls that 'Major Sharp gave an appropriate speech ending with thanks to Jock, who replied in a slightly drunken fashion, but nobody seemed to mind'.[30]

There was much singing and telling of stories well into the night. It was a somewhat strange happening in the proximity of so much suffering and one with which the FAU team were not entirely comfortable.

We were then in the area administered by the 52nd Scottish Lowland Division, and Gordon Taylor writes of the display put on by the Division's Pipes and Drums band:

> Fantastic, probably even enjoyed by the local German folk. The war was over, now Germany could start to get back to some normality. The area included the heavily destroyed cities of Bremen and Hamburg, and they were thankful there would be no more bombing. There were bonfires everywhere, and Very lights shot in the air. Every British soldier was given a booklet from Second Army Command programming the official Thanksgiving Service. I don't recall there being one in our area, but in the larger Army units there were full parades.[31]

But at Sandbostel the celebrations were brief: there was still much to be done. Dennis Wickham's diary continued:

> People are still dying in Camps 1 and 2 at the rate of 20 – 30 a day. Apart from some 1500 who are mostly able to look after themselves, the problem now seems to be essentially a medical one and not for Mil Gov whose responsibility is for Displaced Persons. (9 May)

> Spent most of the day cleaning and disinfecting the Ford ambulance inside and out. (10 May)

Dennis Wickham with his beloved Ford ambulance

This morning went through every barracks and practically every room in Camps 1 and 2. I should think of the remaining inmates some two thirds are still in need of some hospitalisation. There was one poor chap all alone in one room lying on a hard table. One of his legs was like matchsticks, the other from toes to hip was about six times as large and swollen with pus. He was in agony. Len [Darling] left tonight with Colin Sowerbutts in order to recce and prepare a convalescent camp at Seedorf to transfer those inmates who are comparatively fit and able to travel. (11 May)

Len returned this morning. An Army unit had already taken over the camp we intended using. So Len went off again this afternoon to look at another possibility at Farge, north of Bremen. Spent afternoon painting and greasing ambulance. Heard this evening that 500 inmates are to be evacuated tomorrow morning. There was a bulldozer in the camp yesterday digging out yet another mass grave. (12 May)

Crew continues the story of the improvised hospital:

On May 11th, the evacuation to 86 British General Hospital began, just in time to prevent a crisis. From then to May 15th, 1529 new patients were admitted to 10 CCS's hospital and 1382 patients were transferred to 86 BGH, or to a convalescent camp that had just been established by another 30 Corps unit, 3 Field Dressing Station at Seedorf. It was now arranged that 168 Lt Fd Amb working in the camp should not send patients to the hospital before 11 am daily. This gave time for the daily load of transfers to be got away early in the morning. The convalescents for 3 FDS were evacuated during the afternoons when the screening examinations of the patients and inmates of the political prisoners camp was conducted.

The number of typhus cases rose to 600 on May 12th and to 760 on May 16th. The arrival of 8 Mobile Bacteriology Laboratory on May 15th provided a much needed reinforcement. No case of the disease occurred among the personnel of 10 CCS and its associated units. [See comment below.] The patients in the hospital were not permitted to stray beyond the confines of the hospital and visitors were not allowed. Everyone associated with them and all ambulance cars were 'dusted' daily. Separate bathing facilities were provided for the different groups within the hospital population.

On May 17th the last batch of admissions, 92, arrived from the Camp. Since 7 Canadian General Hospital at Bassum had begun to accept transfers on the previous day, the bed state of 10 CCS's hospital began to show a downward trend for the first time since its opening. By May 18th it was down to about 1835, having been 2184 on the 12th, but since only non-typhus cases had been sent to the general hospitals the proportion of typhus cases had grown increasingly larger. With the easing of the burden and the passing of the crisis, sickness among the staff began to increase. The commonest ailment was a febrile, non-specific dysentery. This declined when only watercart water was used for drinking and cooking.[32]

Although, according to Crew, no personnel at 10 CCS caught typhus, members of 168 Lt Fd Amb were not so lucky. Their War Diary records that one of their doctors, a Captain Baker, succumbed to the disease on 17 May and a Major Trott, the second in command, on the 22nd. They were both evacuated to another CCS.[33]

Many of the German helpers also caught the disease. Elfie Walther, one of the high-school girls drafted in from Delmenhorst, wrote in her diary on her return from Sandbostel after twelve days caring for the sick inmates: 'Soon after, at least twenty-five of my school friends went down with typhus, including my friend Rosi. We were injected afterwards. But for many it was too late. Three days after my return, everyone in my house had lice.'[39]

In this respect members of 2 FAU were very fortunate. We all escaped the disease, possibly because we had all been inoculated with an anti-typhus vaccine before leaving England, and no doubt the careful daily dusting with DDT powder helped keep us free of lice.

British Army medical orderly dusts German worker with anti-typhus powder before she leaves the Camp. Photo: Imperial War Museum

German men and women workers leave the Camp at the end of the day's work. Photo: Imperial War Museum

With the convalescent camps set up by 2 FAU at Farge and by 3 FDS at Seedorf both now in operation, and the General Hospital at Bassum accepting patients from 10 CCS's hospital, Crew records that it now became possible to consider closing down the improvised hospital. A start was made on 25 May on the burning of the camp, although a few huts in the political prisoners' compound had been burned several days before the FAU left on 16 May. The staff of the hospital were progressively reduced by the departure of several Army units, the internee doctors and the German nurses. 'By June 3rd the last 350 patients had been evacuated and the hospital wards were empty and silent. A fence enclosed

More German men and women workers leaving the Camp at the end of the day's work. Photo: Imperial War Museum

the cemetery in which a notice commemorating the dead had been erected. Of the rest of those who passed through this hospital very many were shortly to die, for their health had been far too greatly destroyed.'[35]

Back in the political prisoners' camp the work continued until all the inmates had been transferred to the hospital or on to convalescent camps. The PoWs had long gone from their camp. Gordon Taylor records that German men from surrounding towns were brought in to help Army personnel dismantle the huts, and huge mounds of timber were made, which were later burnt. Gordon and I cannot recall anyone attempting to identify the dead, indeed there was no means of doing this, nor was there any form of religious service as the bodies were placed in the pits: this was an urgent and continuous process and a service would have been quite impractical in the circumstances. However, there may have been something of this nature at a later date after we had left the Camp. A new cemetery and memorial was erected some years later, about 2 km from the Camp, and remembrance services are held in the little Camp church. (See Epilogue.)

Each evening we divested ourselves of the protective clothing and returned to our tented camp to eat and sleep. When space in an old

British nursing sister walking with two convalescents at 10 CCS's tented hospital fourteen days after the uncovering of the Camp. Photo: Imperial War Museum

Scene in the cleansed kitchen, 14 May. Photo: Imperial War Museum

German Army barracks became vacant as British Army personnel were withdrawn, it was allocated to the FAU, but the team, rather than taking it for themselves, agreed that the German women who had accompanied us should have the accommodation, a decision the women accepted but found difficult to understand. Because of the tense situation the women were guarded by British soldiers for their own protection. The twelve Polish DPs who had travelled with the FAU/Mil Gov convoy built large fires – there appeared to be surplus wood everywhere – over which large cauldrons were placed which provided a liberal supply of

German workers dig more graves, supervised by British Army personnel, 14 May. Photo: Imperial War Museum

hot water. Although living conditions were somewhat primitive we all seemed to keep reasonably clean and remained in good physical health, if exhausted. Towards the end of our time there an Army bath unit arrived and we all enjoyed a hot shower. Our clothes were washed by some Russian women and we began to feel whole again.

After sixteen days at Sandbostel, 2 FAU moved its base to Farge, north of Bremen on the east bank of the Weser, where we had been helping 205 Mil Gov Det to establish a convalescent camp for some of the slightly fitter ex-inmates from Sandbostel. It was a joy to recognise some of them walking about looking just a little better, although dressed in the most incongruous of clothing. Unfortunately some 150 did not stand up to the journey from Sandbostel in lorries and had to be accommodated in the hospital. I wrote home on 16 May:

The camp is an ex-Kriegsmarine Lager (German Navy Camp). There is a hospital on the site practically fully staffed, with only some one hundred patients, but beds for six hundred! It has been decided to use the trained staff, beds and buildings to look after some of the human wrecks from the improvised hospital at Sandbostel. The hospital kitchen is already preparing food for the convalescent camp. Adjoining the camp building is another truly terrible place, one of the notorious underground 'factories', with the remains of the doings of the SS guards. It is in a great mess amid the signs of the hurried departure of the released 'slave' labourers. The place had been partially blown up and burnt out. From what we have learned it appears the 'slave' labourers lived underground, virtually employed like pit ponies, rarely seeing the light of day. Underground waterways connect with one of the infamous U-boat pens in the river Weser. We assume the 'factory' must have been a U-boat maintenance depot of some sort.

It is strange to get used to seeing German soldiers, still in uniform waiting to be demobilised, just walking about. For a defeated army their uniforms are quite smart and they salute, if rather stiffly, any Allied personnel. In Bremen German police are already on traffic duty directing British Army vehicles through the devastated streets.

We are enduring an early heatwave and it is tiring to keep working in our heavy khaki uniforms. We would love to go for a dip in the river [but this was not advised]. With some relief we have learnt that Army orders now allow battledress tops to be left off, and for officer's shirts and ties worn provided no braces show! Webbing belts to be worn over the top of trousers. I am sure the FAU will be quick to follow suit, but in their own fashion!

We have had some great news. Headquarters 30 Corps have recognised 205 Mil Gov Det's hard work at Sandbostel and have ordered a five-day rest in a suitable place to start as soon as the present job is completed. (16 May)

As work in the convalescent camp is not very heavy with so many other personnel to help now, it has been decided that the 'good news' should be implemented straight away. The FAU team has been split in two. I was in the first half and journeyed to Cuxhaven, a very pleasant, virtually undamaged resort on the north German coast. We were billeted in a German house for two nights. The lady of the house, who lived alone, was wary but not hostile, and was willing to cook our rations for us. We had a splendid time, swimming and sunning ourselves on the beach. One day we went to Neuhaus on the river Oste, where we enjoyed sailing and rowing small boats. However, rowing in just a pair of soccer pants, while good sport, allows the salt air and the sun to burn the skin! It was worth a bit of discomfort though! We returned to Farge today to learn that the whole Bremen area is being turned over to make an enclave for the American Army, so we will be on the move again soon. (21 May)

Even today I can recall those few days of near normality following our harrowing experiences. We had seen sights we wished never to see again and indelible impressions etched into our memories. We were glad to have been available at the right time and to have played our small part in saving many lives. However, this satisfaction was greatly diminished by the knowledge that many lives could not be saved, and there were others whose hurts could not be healed.

CHAPTER 5

The Political Prisoners

Owing mainly to the vast scale, the urgency and intensity of the work and not least the language problem, we had little communication with the internees, apart from their immediate needs. Many were virtually beyond speaking, and most had little inclination to converse. It was clear, however, that they came from many different nationalities. Crew recorded that 'of the 4663 examined in the improvised hospital there were 4 Austrians, 148 Belgians, 1 Canadian, 1 Chinese, 93 Czechs, 1 Danish, 243 Dutch, 2 Estonians, 757 French, 50 Germans, 94 Greeks, 94 Hungarians, 93 Italians, 134 Latvians, 26 Lithuanians, 1 Luxembourger, 994 Poles, 6 Rumanians, 1828 Russians, 20 Spaniards, and 73 Yugoslavs'.[36] Those who remained in the original compound were slightly fitter and did not go through the improvised hospital, but were transferred after a time directly to the convalescent camps. They were equally heterogeneous, but no exact record was made.

The political prisoners had come from all walks of life and included university lecturers, physicians, architects, lawyers, businessmen, a sculptor and habitual criminals. But all had come into conflict with the Nazi regime in one way or another. Some had been taken from home as forced labour and then placed immediately into a concentration camp or been caught after attempting to run away from the place of employment. Some were prisoners of war from PoW camps taken for labour, in contravention of the Geneva Red Cross Convention, and thereafter treated as civilians and sent to a concentration camp. Some had been taken from prison during or at the end of their sentences, some were arrested because of their political views, others arrested as members of resistance groups, or having been found in possession of weapons following the uprising in Warsaw, a few were arrested simply because they were Jews.

Apart from the Russian and Poles, one of the larger groupings was the French, many of whom had been in the Resistance movement, and seemed the most organised. But it was from members of the Dutch Resistance, several of whom had good English, that we learnt some of what had happened. The inmates had been in Sandbostel only for some four weeks, brought there cramped in cattle wagons, dead and dying amongst them, from the concentration camp at Neuengamme, near Hamburg. None had expected to survive. Just before they departed, two SS guards had fired with their machine guns at some of the internees who were attempting to raid the kitchen for food. Many gunshot wounds found among the survivors testified to the truth of this. Apparently the Wehrmacht (German Army) guards took no steps to prevent either the raiding of the stores or the machine gunning by the SS. Later, when most of the SS and German Army guards withdrew, as the British forces advanced, the running of the Camp was taken over by French prisoners from the PoW camp, but there was little they could do but await the arrival of the British Army.

Crew has written of the transport of the prisoners to Sandbostel:

They had been transferred to Sandbostel for extermination. Some 9000 of them arrived by rail in open cattle trucks, 100 to a truck, after a journey lasting 8 days, during which they were without water and food, and were never permitted to leave the trucks. Some 2000 were dead on arrival. Those who could move were made to march the 2 km to the camp. Those who could not, being either dead or else too weak, were bundled into small sand-carrying tip trucks and taken by narrow rail to the Camp, where they were tipped in heaps to lie until their fellows came to fetch them. This was between 13 – 18 April. Between then and 1st of May their deliberate elimination proceeded. The seeds of typhus and respiratory tuberculosis were widely sown as malnutrition, gross overcrowding, and complete absence of any measure of environmental sanitation produced their dire effects.[37]

As described earlier, two PoWs, an Englishman and a Frenchman, had escaped the Camp and managed to find their way to the lines of the Guards Armoured Division, carrying a message for help. This read:

To: Local Commander British Forces

From: Service Officer Allied Prisoners of War

Tragic state of affairs at the camp at Sandbostel. Seven thousand political prisoners of all nationalities from a concentration camp are in dangerously low state of health and are in need of immediate help. Fourteen thousand Allied prisoners of war of all nationalities of whom 1500 are ill, need help. Colonel Albert of the French Army has already taken over complete control of the camp, this has been mutually arranged with the German authorities. Please come to relief of the camp, it will be handed over without any resistance.

Signed: Albert

Both PoWs and political prisoners were heartened by an immediate answer dropped from an aircraft over the Camp: 'Courage and Hope. Help comes.'[38]

The SS had left the Camp several days earlier, and the German Army guards who were left were more than willing to surrender. They had in fact turned over the running of the Camp to the French PoWs. However, the German units in the surrounding area were not so amenable and put up very fierce resistance, and British soldiers suffered very heavy casualties liberating the Camp. Their sacrifice should not be forgotten in this story, for by turning aside to rescue the Camp several days earlier than would otherwise have been the case, many lives were saved among the political prisoners by the earlier treatment that became possible.

Many of those who survived into the convalescent camps had developed psychological problems. M.C. Carey, who visited both 10 CCS's improvised hospital at Sandbostel and 86 BGH at Rotenburg, some 20 miles to the south, to which some of the patients had been transferred, has written at some length on this aspect.[39] Towards the end of his article he writes:

A few days of hospital treatment and kindness, however, produce a dramatic change, though the men still tend to hoard food. After every meal the nurses will find bread or even bowls of soup hidden away under pillows and mattresses. The first issue of pyjamas is always a great occasion. The men have not been really clean and shaved or had fresh clothing for many months. One of them still too weak to stand alone, insisted on being helped by an orderly to stagger across the ward, to show himself off to the others in his new pyjamas.

When the Ward Sister brought a vase of flowers and green leaves into the ward for the first time it had to be so placed that everyone could see it. By next morning a number of leaves were missing. Several of the patients had crawled out of bed and taken the leaves, which they had put beside them on the pillows. The Sister asked a man why he had done this. 'They are so pretty. I wanted to have them close to me', he replied.

Carey goes on to describe the extraordinary effect on morale of the visit of the Red Cross Welfare worker attached to the hospital. 'The moment she went into a ward there was a general turning of heads and a heightening of interest amongst those well enough to recognise her.' Although they hoped she might bring biscuits or cigarettes, both in very short supply, it was clearly not only this.

She talked to them of home and of the outside world. At first they took little interest in when they were likely to be well enough to get home again. They did not seem to be able to realise that this would ever be possible. But gradually the question, 'When shall I get home?' had to be translated for all the different languages.

The Red Cross worker taught them to say 'Please' and 'Thank you' again. They were like children about this, and brought out the words with smiles and gestures of gratitude. They loved the personal touch, the feeling that someone was really interested in them. Gradually civilised instincts of a former life began to assert themselves, and those who eventually survive the ravages of tuberculosis may ultimately get back to normality or very nearly so.

Carey describes leaving the hospital: 'Outside the long tent, in which the atmosphere was heavy with the smell of disease and death, a soft air was blowing, and the sun was breaking through after torrential thunder showers. Then a lark went up. How great a contrast with the scene I had just left, broken and murdered humanity in such a lovely world.'

CHAPTER 6

The German Helpers

Apart from the sixty to seventy young German women who travelled with the FAU/Mil Gov convoy, many other German people, including doctors and nurses but also many general helpers, were drafted in from the surrounding towns and villages to help clear up the Camp. Some lived on the site in huts or tents, but others were brought in on a daily basis, and in a few days they outnumbered the British personnel.

For the same reasons as with the political prisoners, as explained earlier – pressure of the work and language difficulties – we FAU had little communication with the German women, apart from immediate matters to do with the work, and so learnt little of their feelings. In any case they were mostly hesitant to talk in the early days, which was understandable; and although the FAU did not subscribe to the non-fraternisation rule, it did not make it any easier. The tasks the German women and nurses had to undertake were highly dangerous, because of the widespread typhus, but they were so horrified by what they saw that they worked willingly.

While I was researching for this book it became clear that it would be a more complete and balanced story if I could include the experiences of a few of the German helpers. So on 18 May 1997 I placed a brief notice in the *Weser-Kurier*, a newspaper that circulates in and around Bremen, requesting anyone who had helped at the Sandbostel camp to write to me with their experiences and reactions. I had only nine replies, but after 52 years such a small number was not unexpected.

I do not know to what extent local German people were involved in clearing up other concentration camps in Germany, but in reading accounts it does not seem to me that recognition has always been made of the enormous help given by people living in the vicinity. Of course, they were drafted labour brought in partly as a form of 'education'. But it is very doubtful whether the rescue work could have been done so quickly but for this help, and lives were saved that otherwise would not have been.

All who wrote to me expressed horror and shame that German people could have committed these atrocities, and are adamant that these things should never be allowed to happen again anywhere in the world. In some way my notice in the newspaper seems to have been an opportunity for them to write down feelings that they had long had but been unable to express before – a recognition, even a release. Inevitably the letters to me covered very similar ground, so I have had to be very selective in making the following extracts.

***Ilse Schröder from Bremen* wrote:**

We girls were all in our early twenties, and the order transmitted by the German police to prepare ourselves with a small amount of baggage frightened us. The war was not yet over and, although as conquered enemies we were told very little, we knew that fighting still continued around Hamburg. The journey to the camp on the night of 1 May was very depressing and frightening. We saw many dead bodies, both soldiers and civilians, lying in the streets and we were often passed by lorries of German soldiers who had been taken prisoner. The arrival at the Camp was a deep shock when we saw for the first time the hungry, starved faces. We knew nothing of the horrors of these places, which had been referred to only as camps for foreign workers.

To the side of the main camp were several wooden barracks in which the German guards had lived. These we made clean, beds were put up and straw sacks filled, in preparation for the sick people. Under the eyes of English soldiers the emaciated bodies had to be washed and deloused. By evening, we girls were utterly exhausted, shaken by shame and revulsion. We were accommodated in one of the barracks and slept on mattresses or field beds. Later I was sent to work in the big kitchen and had to distribute food to the Camp inmates. There we could talk a little with the English personnel and the French cooks, who had been prisoners of war in the camp nearby. The English treated us with extreme coldness but always very correctly. After a drunken soldier intruded into our barracks at night, guards were placed at the door. We were treated daily with delousing powder till our hair was quite white.

Every day the weaker inmates died and were buried in mass graves by local people, who were very shocked by the extent of the horror that had been taking place so near to where they lived, they could not believe it. Bit by bit the Camp was liquidated. Some girls were taken home after about fourteen days, but those of us who worked in the kitchen stayed a little longer. The whole experience had a deep and long lasting effect on me. I was ashamed of the deeds of my fellow countrymen, and sad and disillusioned at the collapse of my country. In the Hitler Youth we had heard only of the good and noble things and our belief was deeply shattered. It was a long time ago but should not be forgotten, and now there is more hope that such things will never be repeated. I find it wonderful that you are wanting to document the events at Sandbostel and wish you well with your book.

Maria von Reinken from Bremen wrote:

For about fourteen days in May 1945 I was a Red Cross assistant in Sandbostel. About ten other helpers travelled with me in a British Army lorry on a journey for which we were in no way prepared. We did not know the object of the exercise or whether we would ever come home again. None of us knew of the existence of Sandbostel Camp. When we arrived much had already been organised in our part of the Camp. Each sick and dying person had his own bed, a shirt and a blanket, and some sanitary arrangements had been installed as far as this was possible. Some German nurses who had been there some time came to us weeping of what they had seen in the first days. There were English and German doctors and English medical orderlies among other helpers. Medicines and food were being provided through the British Army. Cleaned barracks had been made available and a large tent for medical examination had been erected. During the following days I saw many very sick and emaciated people, and also many who had died.

I still have two letters that I sent at the time to people in Bremen, and in them I wrote that I was looking after Poles and Russians. I still remember their haunted faces. From these letters it emerges clearly that none of us understood the significance of what had happened. To me it was just another experience in the bewildering chronicle of events of the war years, like the day and night bombing of Bremen, and finally a few days before we left for Sandbostel the capitulation of our city.

I am unable to detail in any way the days in the Camp, we simply got on with the work before us. Each evening we helpers met in a field and read from a book of poetry that one of us had hidden in a pocket of her skirt, none of us had any bags or cases. We encouraged each other and exchanged practical hints. We knew nothing about the sick people or what became of them. After our return to Bremen a few of us helpers met each other on a few occasions, but then lost touch.

Marianne Martens, who was a general helper from Seedorf, wrote:

Every year in May and June I think back to our journey to Sandbostel and what we saw and experienced there. I am now old and my writing is shaky, but I still write every week to my sister in Canada – she emigrated there with her husband and two children in 1955. We came every three days with about 35 other men and women from our little village of Seedorf. I was only twenty-two years old at the time. We were collected by a British Army lorry at 8 in the morning. On our first day we were met by a friendly Englishman at the entrance to the Camp, and after a long walk we arrived at a carpentry workshop. Here we carried planks for the building of toilets, which were very badly needed. We were dusted frequently with delousing powder, but I did not do any actual nursing. We helped erect tents for those weak but recovering people. In the main camp we helped clean up, scrubbed beds, filled straw sacks for bedding, or did any other work that was necessary. Each time my sister visits from Canada we go to the graves at Sandbostel and attend the service in the Camp church. We also go there on the day of national mourning, but as one grows older this is less frequent. I am sorry I have not been able to write more fully, but I assure you I have seen all the horrors. Such things must never, ever be allowed to happen again anywhere in the world.

Rosemarie Kirmse, who worked in the improvised hospital, writes from Bremen:

> On 7 May 1945 a German policeman came to our house and told me that I was to report on the following morning at 8 am at the School Am Barkhof. About fifty girls all aged between eighteen and twenty-four years old set out for the Police headquarters not knowing what was in store for us. Three similar groups from other districts of Bremen were already gathered there. We waited for several hours but finally between 2 or 3 in the afternoon lorries arrived which we had to get into. Before embarking I asked an elderly married couple who were watching the event to tell my parents I would probably not come home that day. When we arrived at Sandbostel we were not allowed to disembark at once, but then some happy German girls came up to us. Some days before they had been taken to the Camp by English soldiers who had occupied Delmenhorst, and were now being allowed to go home. Suddenly we saw some men dressed only in grey blankets, only skin and bones, who had come out to enjoy the sun in the first warm day. The sight of these men terrified us. We got out of the lorries and were counted; there were 179 of us.

> We were assigned to individual barracks, mine was Block D, everywhere there was a terrible smell. We were inoculated against typhus as almost all the inmates had the disease. We worked from 8 in the morning till 7 in the evening, with a midday break of one and a half hours. We were given breakfast, midday and evening meals, but only after the patients had eaten. I got on well with the

26 patients whom I had to look after in two rooms. Most were Dutch, some French and Belgians and a seventeen-year-old who called me 'Mummy', he had lost his mother and sisters in another concentration camp. I was twenty-one years old at the time. At midday there was usually a one-pot meal and I was surprised that these sick people were able to digest this rough food. During the hot days there was a problem with the patients' fluid intake and we collected and filled mugs with fruit juice so that they would have something for the night. Apart from distributing the food and carrying the dirty crockery to the kitchen, I was continually on the move bringing out and cleaning pails and chamber pots. There was only time to shake up the mattresses containing straw occasionally; when I did this it produced a cloud of dust but the faces of 'my patients' shone with pleasure.

After two weeks a start was made to replace the wooden double-decker bunks with proper hospital beds. Then bed linen and pyjamas were provided. Gradually those patients who were able to walk a little were transported to a convalescent hospital at Farge. Many did not want to go there, and it was only recently that I learnt that many of them had worked there as forced labour under terrible conditions, which explained their reluctance.

The staff nurse in charge of Block D was an Englishwoman, and when my shoes completely wore out, she went with me to a little hut full of soldiers' boots, but none of these fitted me, so we returned without having had any luck. In the kitchen I met Joseph, an English soldier who was helping us, I think he may have been a medical orderly. We all got on well with him and when he saw the state of my shoes he at once quite spontaneously took off his own black shoes and gave them to me. They fitted very well. He explained he could obtain a replacement pair without difficulty. You see, Mr Barnard, I have never forgotten this friendly gesture in such difficult circumstances. This little occurrence is probably not important, but I am glad to be able to tell the story to an Englishman after so many years.

After about two weeks I was moved to another bigger ward under the charge of a German nurse. Here the patients were even more ill, and some still dying. They were not aware of what had happened and some still stammered, 'Heil Hitler'. I was very worried for them. I had never before seen a person dying, but here I saw many bodies carried out with a label tied to their big toe. Many of us girls had to help to dig graves all the time we were at Sandbostel. One patient was in a single room and the door was always left open, as any female person answering his call was immediately dragged on to his bed. I experienced this.

After about two weeks I was allowed to go to Bremen in a British Red Cross vehicle to fetch some clean clothes and toilet articles. I was allowed only two hours, so I rushed from the big hospital to my home and surprised my very worried parents with my sudden appearance. In Bremen most extraordinary rumours were circulating about what had happened to us. I packed up my few things and hurried back to the hospital accompanied by my mother. It was wonderful to be able at last to wash myself properly and clean my teeth. However, I never got accustomed to sleeping on a very narrow folding bed. Gradually more and more German nurses arrived. They had been looking after things in the actual concentration camp, which we were not allowed to enter. After some four to five weeks our help was no longer needed and we were brought back to Bremen in British Red Cross vehicles.

It was a terrible experience that I shall never forget, so I am grateful that I have found in you a person to whom I can write about these experiences, because you, I know, will understand. Unfortunately, I was unable to attend the service which took place here about two years ago in the Chapter House of the Cathedral to commemorate Sandbostel, as I was unwell.

Ingeborg Wark from Bremen wrote:

As a qualified nurse I worked during1944 and 1945 in the emergency hospital at Untersted, near Rotenburg, which was attached to the Bremen Municipal Hospital. I worked in the Diphtheria section, but on 8 May this was reduced to one small wooden house, while the other buildings were cleaned and disinfected. Then British soldiers arrived and we were made a part of 86 British General Hospital. As the last German patients were moved out, British medical vehicles brought in the new patients, victims from the concentration camp at Sandbostel. Most were so weak they had to be carried to their beds and almost all had continual diarrhoea: because of this they could not wear trousers. Sixty patients now occupied our buildings and we were only three nurses. Because of the military activity we had no running water and only emergency lighting. One nurse fetched water in cans from a spring, another made sandwiches and distributed tea, and the third put patients over a basin to clean them after evacuation from diarrhoea. They were very difficult first days. More and more patients arrived in the following days, till the buildings became overcrowded and tents had to be erected. Fortunately more nursing personnel, including some German PoWs, were brought in to assist. An English nurse had supervision over each section. Soon about a thousand patients were looked after in the hospital, but in the first weeks many died, probably a hundred a day, through the result of malnutrition, diarrhoea, bronchitis, and so on. It was a constant coming and going, but gradually the state of the patients improved and they were released. By August 1945 we still had just twelve patients left who were in reasonably good health and were looked after by the exhausted nurses with pleasure. Some of the patients who had co-operated with the Camp authorities as supervisors and so on (Kapos) were kept in a separate barracks and guarded by British soldiers. They were hated very much by the other patients, who would probably have lynched them if they could have done. The patients came from many nationalities, but I can remember Dutch, Belgians, French, Hungarians and Russians, but also one or two Germans. We attempted to communicate through the help of those patients who could speak some German. Many times I enquired where they had come from and was always told from Sandbostel, an extension of the concentration camp at Neuengamme. These names were completely strange to us and we had no idea of the conditions in them.

Anne Loesche from Bremen wrote:

As a qualified nursing sister with a knowledge of French and English I was allocated to a barracks with about a hundred double-decker bunks with straw mattresses. In the first days the patients had little to eat and the only crockery to feed them with was one cup and one spoon. There was a bucket in the middle of the room which served as a toilet. An English doctor was in charge, assisted by two Russian doctors. I had a Red Cross trainee and a young girl to help me. She and the other young ladies from the better-off quarters of Bremen were quite untrained for this work, and Sandbostel was a severe shock to them. Several had nervous breakdowns and had to be taken home to Bremen. The relatives of these young girls did not know what had happened to them and did not have any news. At first I found it difficult to understand these harsh measures for we had known nothing of these atrocities. The Allied troops entering Germany had seen the consequences of unheard-of barbarism and acted accordingly. They had great difficulties to overcome. I became an involuntary witness to this terrible time. Although I have no wish to remove the experience from my life's memory, I still find it difficult to believe that there really were such camps and that so much human degradation took place in them. At the time I was very shattered and depressed. This did not escape the notice of our English doctor, and after two weeks she invited my sister, who was working in another barracks, to tea, where the Russian doctors divided up the cake, which they ate with us.

Beyond their immediate physical needs it was not easy to help many of the patients. It is difficult to describe what hunger can do to human beings. All natural control disappears, but what a miracle there is when those people get better – it is like a rebirth. I learnt much from them and how they had come to be in Sandbostel. One young Frenchman had only just been married before he was taken for forced labour in Germany. Twice he escaped to flee in the direction of France in a longing to see his wife, but he was recaptured and on the second occasion sent to a concentration camp. His only remaining possession was a small keepsake with a photo of his wife, which he showed me proudly. My little cat he called her. Sadly he was too weak to recover and died later. How gladly I would have written to his wife but we had no address and did not even know his name. There was also a German pharmacist from Berlin whose two sons were killed at the front and then his wife died when his house was destroyed in an air raid. In his despair he lost all caution and began to curse Hitler and all his works. He was betrayed by a neighbour and taken to a concentration camp, but he survived all the conditions to regain much of his health, but what had he to live for? There were some in the camp because they had committed crimes, such as robbing the army mail. Much suffering was caused by the

'Kapos', men who co-operated with the Camp authorities and had been promoted to supervise the inmates, for privileges. They were much hated and, after the liberation of the Camp, Polish officers were designated to seek them out.

Disease was rife throughout the Camp – typhus, diarrhoea, bronchitis, but particularly tuberculosis. However, many did begin to recover from their ordeal and were moved to convalescent hospitals in the surrounding district. The British authorities provided endless supplies. Who knows how much hard work it took to discover and bring in to the Camp – blankets, clothing, night wear, crockery, and medicines. It was an extraordinary achievement which was carried out in such a short time. We nurses had to work round the clock and didn't know what day of the week it was. We were so happy when a patient showed signs of recovery from the hell in which he had lived.

The days passed in monotonous activity of practical work, but one evening we felt something special must have happened. We learnt later that it was the evening of 8 May, and the Allied troops were celebrating the end of the war. However, the work went on relentlessly and 'Peace' was not a word we found easy to use. I was nineteen years old when the war started and I was twenty-five now it had stopped, but we knew with a sense of relief that the killing was now over.

Towards the end I still had one room at Sandbostel with about twenty French patients to look after, all well on the way to recovery, and waiting to be repatriated to France. I don't think they appreciated how much of the language I could understand. But on one day their talk was all of hatred and revenge, but one young French teacher said, 'Not all Germans were like that. There were also some decent humane people even among the guards. You must be just, for that is peace.'

I very much welcome that you as a member of the Friends Ambulance Unit are planning to write a book about the operation to rescue the people of Sandbostel Camp, and I hope what I have written will help you. I wish you success in your work to prevent these things being forgotten. May there always be people who are prepared, each in their own way, to take action against crimes towards humanity.

As the Camp ran down, Gordon Taylor recalled how he took some of the women back to Delmenhorst in his truck. His orders from Mil Gov were to drop them off in the town centre, not their homes, but Gordon did his best to get them as near as possible, though he had very little conversation with them. They were all still shocked at what they had experienced, some were sick, all worn out, and did not wish to communicate, but they had all worked without restraint to the point of exhaustion.

CHAPTER 7

After Sandbostel

For the members of 2 FAU Sandbostel was the most traumatic experience of our lives, but there were other desperate situations all around us in war-torn Germany. By involving ourselves with this need we started slowly to work ourselves back to something nearer normality.

On 26 May 2 FAU moved to Hesslingen, near Braunschweig. The town built around the Volkswagen car factory had become a vast displaced persons camp. We had been there only about ten days when another FAU team took over the work, and we moved at short notice to Tangermünde on the Elbe on 5 June. At the time the Elbe was the frontier between the British and Russian zones of occupation. On 9 June I wrote home:

> Our billets are in a house 50 yards from the Elbe, and on the further bank one can see the troops of the Red Army. In fact we have come east as far as we can go. This place is rather historic as it was here that seventy thousand German soldiers, leaving seven thousand burnt out vehicles on the east bank, crossed over, blowing up the bridges behind them in the face of the advancing Russians,

and surrendered to five American soldiers. In a way our work is going to be a bit historic too. A pontoon bridge has been constructed across the river, with bunting and flags and appropriate guards at each end, with a barrier in the middle. One half of the bridge is painted red, and the other half red, white and blue. Across this bridge each day we are passing groups of Russian DPs and in return we are receiving Western nationals, mainly French and Dutch. We are running a small transit camp in the town for people to sleep overnight before going east or west.

The War Diary of 205 Mil Gov Det records on 26 June:

> The Russian Major in charge of the DP camp across the Elbe visited our camps by arrangement at his request. After the visit he told the Russian Liaison Officers attached to 205 Det that he had been very pleased with his reception by officers of the Detachment and with the care of Russian DPs and PoWs in the camps. The total of PoWs and men of military age evacuated across the Elbe was 11,272 and 5340 DPs. Total westbound DPs who crossed from the Russian side was 139.[40]

Also from my letter of 9 June:

> Tangermünde is perhaps the prettiest German town I have seen so far, with no damage that I have seen. It is here that the river Tanger flows into the Elbe. It was a river port, but did not handle enough trade for industry to spoil its charm. There are delightful cobblestoned streets leading down to the river bank and many of the houses are a half wooden timbered type, with green bottle glass

windows. From shops hang beautifully carved wooden signs. It was a walled city, and several arches and little towers remain. But perhaps most typically German of all was a stork's nest on top of the Rathaus [town hall].

Tangermünde on the river Elbe, June 1945, at the time the border between the British and Russian zones of occupation. Russian and Ukrainian DPs with their belongings being assembled before being sent into the Russian zone. Note the destroyed railway bridge in the background which had carried the main line to Berlin.

After four weeks Tangermünde became part of the Russian zone and we had to move again to Buxtehude, north of Hamburg, and then later to Otterndorf, near Cuxhaven, almost on the coast, where we had little to do. At this time I became due for home leave and had twelve very

Russian and Ukrainian DPs crossing a temporary pontoon footbridge over the Elbe from British to Russian zones of occupation on their way home. A very small red star can just be seen over the arch at the far end of the bridge.

welcome days with my parents at home. Several older members of the team became eligible for release and returned home and we were joined by others from England.

At the end of August the team moved again to the little village of Dünsen, some 25 km south of Bremen. Here we had been asked by Mil Gov to convert an old army camp into winter quarters for Polish DPs. The camp was situated on the edge of a forest with many brick and wooden buildings dotted about. It had been surrounded by a minefield but this, we were assured, had just been cleared. Groups of some four hundred local German men were drafted in to make habitable as many of the buildings as possible, clear the debris and make the roads passable. The first thousand Poles were moved in quite quickly, and we were kept busy organising supplies and arranging facilities for what was to become virtually a little 'town'. Fortunately we had two nice brick houses as billets, which we thought would see us through the winter, and we made ourselves comfortable for a longer than usual stay. I wrote home:

> During the clearing up we found a cat and five little kittens in a dark, damp cellar. They were all in a rather poor condition. I can't imagine how the mother cat had managed for food, as no one had been in the place, except the soldiers who had cleared the mines, since the fighting ceased four months ago. The cat must have been a good hunter. The kittens could hardly be more than a week old. So we took the whole family into our quarters and fed them up. Now there are kittens everywhere, little balls of fluffy mischief. (31 August)

We are very busy at the moment, as about 1600 Polish people have now arrived. It is rather like running a housing estate which has to try to be self-contained. Everything possible has to be thought of for the coming winter. Most of the buildings were in a bad state of disrepair: drains, water and electricity supplies had to be got going. Although the Poles formed labouring groups, the more expert work has had to be found from among the local German population, and brought in daily with very limited transport. A hundred and one authorities, British, American and German, have had to be negotiated with to release coal and wooden fuel, food, cleaning and medical supplies to ensure sufficient quantities for the whole winter. It is still not known how many we shall finally have to cater for as new arrivals come in all the time. A complete community is getting going but already they have a school for two hundred children, a church with a Sunday school, nursery school, adult school, hospital with outpatients clinic, child welfare clinic, pig and poultry farms, PT classes, a fire brigade, police force, communal laundry, a colossal central kitchen, cinema, theatre, dance hall, and so on. Scout and Girl Guide troops and a soccer club have been started. There is also a gardening scheme, a bit like the allotments at home. The Poles are mostly enthusiastic and co-operative, staffing all these activities themselves, but supplies of everything are so short. Most things have to be obtained from German sources, but piles of red tape have to be gone through first.

The other evening we were formally invited by the Camp Entertainment Committee to the opening dance. As we arrived the music stopped, the floor cleared and we walked across the room to be met in the middle by the Polish Major, commandant of the camp, and other officials, who saluted, clicked heels and shook hands. We were then conducted to a corner of the room marked off by bushes in tubs, where the Major delivered a welcome speech in English. We sat down at small tables and smoked cigarettes and drank something we supposed was coffee with the Major and his company. Dancing renewed and obviously picked girls hovered near at hand should we wish to dance. The band was surprisingly good, but the dancing was rather different to what we were accustomed to – fox-trots, slow waltzes and tangos are all mixed into one dance, which is repeated continually with no breaks! Later there was a display, by six girls and six men in high boots, of a Polish version of 'cossack' dancing. There is never a dull moment in a relief worker's life! (9 September)

Recently we had an inspection by a British Army Brigadier, who was favourably impressed at the progress and standard the camp had achieved. Bill Barnes, the FAU team leader at the time, explained our problems with supplies of all kinds, and that same evening we got some equipment and have been receiving many wanted items ever since. We are officially called a Polish Community Estate now. (15 September)

We are now carrying out a complete registration of every person in the camp in connection with repatriation. However, it is far from clear whether this will happen before the winter or next spring. We have heard unofficially that the British Control Commission would like to get all the Polish people who lived west of the Curzon Line back to their homes before the end of the year, but it is apparent that most of those who used to live east of the line, now occupied by the Russians, do not want to go at all. (19 September)

The Curzon Line was the proposed Eastern frontier of Poland recognised by the Allies in 1919, but not adopted as a boundary between Poland and Russia in consequence of the former's victory over the latter in

1920. The line became a virtual reality as Poland's eastern frontier in 1945, having been accepted as a basis for the future demarcation at the Tehran Conference in 1943 by Russia, Britain and the USA. On 23 September I wrote home:

> Work in the camp goes on apace. A few more buildings have had to be cleaned and rehabilitated, and our capacity continues to go up. We are trying to gather every Polish national from the surrounding countryside into the camp before the winter sets in. A few of the wooden huts were past repairing and are now being pulled down for firewood. Owing to the large numbers of people now in the camp, the sanitation system broke down and we had to organise work parties to dig up the drains in parts of the camp and lay more pipes. What a job! We are rather isolated here being the only British unit for some miles around, and the neighbouring villages look upon us as the official administration, which has led to some amusing incidents. A Greek doctor, who had lived in Germany for some time, came in to see us. He thought because he was an allied national he should now be made the Director of the local hospital instead of the present German incumbent. He was a bit put out that we could not effect the change!

In January 1946 our work with DPs came to a close when the team moved to Hannover to take up work mainly concerned with welfare and youth organisation. With the cessation of hostilities the voluntary societies had moved more relief teams into Germany from England. They were at first mostly concerned with the care of DPs. However, it had become increasingly clear that the situation among the German population was worsening, and in the following months several relief teams became engaged with this growing need.

Some members of 2 FAU outside their billet in Ganghöferstrasse, Hannover, January 1946. Left to right, Gordon Taylor, David Davies, the author and James Atkins

2 FAU, as one of the first, was glad to take on this new involvement, although it was a departure from what the team had been doing and new skills had to be learnt on the job. We started by undertaking for Mil Gov a complete survey of all the hospitals, clinics, homes for disabled people and similar institutions, and listed all the existing youth

The author in the Harz mountains on the road to Clausthal-Zellerfeld while researching for a school feeding scheme, July 1946

movements in the city. The Hitler Youth had, of course, been disbanded, and the British Control Commission, who administered the British Zone of Occupation, did not permit the formation of Scout troops as they were considered too paramilitary. Several local youth clubs had, however, been established, some by the churches. While these were mostly being run as well as the prevailing conditions allowed, there was desperate need for supplies of all kinds. We found we could play an effective role liaising between the various British and German local government authorities and the organisations. Tuberculosis was very prevalent, and as a preventative measure we drew up a scheme with Mil Gov and the German authorities to evacuate groups of children from the worst hit areas of Hannover to the Friesian Islands for five weeks at a time. Extra rations were obtained through the Swedish Red Cross. It was hoped that better food and fresh air would help build up resistance to the disease when the children had to return to overcrowded, war-damaged accommodation. On 26 May I wrote home:

> I travelled on a specially arranged train which left Hannover central station at 8 pm on Monday with nine hundred children and many helpers. I shared a compartment with some of the German organisers, Herr Mund from the Gesundheitsamt (Health Office), Pastor Schwedhelm of the Innere Mission (Home Mission, Protestant welfare organisation), an official from the Deutsches Rotes Kreuz (German Red Cross), and two nuns from Caritas Verband (Catholic welfare organisation). The conditions on the train, which only crept along over damaged track, were very bad. Little glass in the windows, mostly wood or even cardboard, and consequently little ventilation, very insanitary and no light

whatsoever. These, mind you, are normal conditions for trains at present, it is amazing there are any trains and track to run them on at all. It was most unsuitable for these far from healthy children, aged between five and thirteen, and the nurses and helpers had a very difficult time.

Although we arrived at 8.30 the following morning it took most of the day to ship the children across the water in air-sea rescue type launches, although it was not far. Langeoog, the island that had been chosen, has a population of about six hundred, and is quite undamaged. Every other building seems to be an hotel or guest house. Before the war the island's main occupation was catering for the tourist trade. Although we have nearly a thousand children there is still room for more. The island is mostly sand dunes, and has lovely beaches. Unfortunately, it rained most of the time I was there so I didn't see it at its best. John [Tanner] came up by car with other German officials, Baroness von Knigge [Deutsches Rotes Kreuz], Dr Meyer and Dr Depuhl, who are both important people in Hannover. Being the only British on the island John and I lived with the German officials in a hotel provided for us. Although we had brought some rations with us we insisted on sharing them and eating the same as the German people. This went down very well. We also had a lot of fish caught locally, and omelettes made from seagulls' eggs! Milk seemed to be in reasonably good supply. Arrangements have been made for the children to receive a good 2000 calories a day. We were shown all the accommodation for the children and inspected the kitchens, which were good by current standards. All the helpers are having to work very hard, caring for the children and arranging activities. On our last evening at supper Dr Depuhl made a short speech thanking us for making the exercise possible and for all the help we had given, and presented us both with the Langeoog badge. [There may have been an omission in this letter, for my recollection is that Roger Stanger was also with us on the island.]

It had been arranged that John and I would stay on the island for three days to make sure everything was running smoothly. On returning to Hannover we wrote a report for Mil Gov on the scheme, suggesting that for future groups travelling might be improved by using fleets of buses in daylight hours on successive days, scheduled to fit in with the tides, which would help to eliminate the delays and save the children waiting with little cover for long periods on the quayside. While warmly received, the idea could not be implemented through lack of buses, none being able to be released from the hard-pressed service in Hannover where there were insufficient anyway. However, the original scheme operated throughout the summer and we were delighted to have been able to initiate it. In a similar venture, Martin Southwood arranged with the help of local German welfare organisations to establish a 'Quaker Erholungsheim' (convalescent home) for undernourished children in Bockswiese in the Harz mountains, which received warm praise from Mil Gov. It was in Hannover too that I met Renate, my wife-to-be.

The FAU closed down in June 1946. Progressively, most of the longer-serving members had been leaving to take up their civilian occupations or return to their studies. The work of the FAU section in Hannover was taken over by a Friends Relief Service team. Some FAU members remaining in Germany transferred to FRS, some returned to England to join the FAU Post War Service, while others like myself transferred to British Red Cross relief teams to carry on similar work in other parts of Germany. This enabled me to continue to fulfil the conditions of my exemption under the National Service Act, until my demobilisation number came up on 25 June 1947.

I was posted towards the end of June to British Red Cross Relief Section 146 which was based at the time in Hildesheim, a small, badly damaged town south of Hannover. While I knew the work would be similar to that which I had been doing, I was not sure how different the approach would be and what the set-up would be like. It was difficult to leave the warm comradeship of the FAU for the unknown. What would their attitude be towards a conscientious objector? I need not have worried.

The British Red Cross team was a new one and had come out from England only five months previously. Things had not worked out. The members had had little training, and the attitude of some of the members to the work left something to be desired. The team leader had been asked to resign, and four other members were transferred to different Sections. BRC HQ hoped to strengthen the team and a new leader was appointed: Ron Hodson, who was a Quaker and an ex-FAU member, with three other ex-FAU members, Frank Taylor, Robin Roberts and Dennis Berry, in addition to myself. So a familiar atmosphere and way of working was soon established. The Section was completed by three women members, a nurse, a teacher, and a social worker, which gave a very helpful dimension to the work. Unfortunately, Ron Hodson had to resign soon after following an attack of jaundice and suspected TB. He had been working among DPs in the damaged Ruhrgebiet for many months. He was replaced by Dennis Ward, an older man, who had been working with a Salvation Army Relief Section before transferring to the British Red Cross. With the ending of the war the 'First Aid' nature of the work had slowly turned to more long term projects, and this was even more in evidence in what the Red Cross team undertook. The FAU team was, perhaps, a little more democratic, but in the event I found little difference in the way the work was handled.

The BRC Section was responsible for a very large area, a whole Regierungs-Bezirk (county) consisting of fifteen Kreise, (local government districts), extending from Göttingen and Hanoversch Munden in the south to Peine in the north. This was a quite unrealistic area to cover adequately, although two other Relief Sections, an FRS team and a Salvation Army one, operated in the area, but both were engaged on quite specific projects. There were several parts of the area that were not visited at all in our time there.

I was asked to carry out a nutritional survey, with Dennis Berry, in the district of Clausthal-Zellerfeld in the Harz mountains, bordering on the Russian zone in the southeast. Although the area was virtually undamaged, the population had been greatly swollen by an influx of refugees and children without parents who had been evacuated from the bombed cities during the war and had nowhere to return to. Many of the houses in the town had been converted into temporary homes for TB patients. At this time the food ration for the German population had been reduced to its lowest level, around 1000 calories a day, although it was later raised to nearer 1500 calories in the winter. The British Control Commission had decided that the ration for children in urban areas should be slightly higher than in rural areas, on the assumption that those in the country districts could supplement their ration a little from locally grown produce. Although the district of Clausthal Zellerfeld was mainly heavily worked hills and agriculture was virtually non-existent, it had been designated as a rural area. But there was no way the ration could be supplemented. Dennis and I visited the whole area and inspected all the schools, finding most of the children in a poor state of health, many without shoes or socks, some wearing crude wooden clogs made locally.

Our report convinced the Control Commission, and the ration was quickly raised to the level of the cities through a school-feeding scheme. The head of the German Red Cross in Clausthal Zellerfeld, a Herr Jünge, and the Oberkreisdirektor, who had been trying to get this recognition for over three months, were overjoyed at the news. They shook us warmly by the hand saying: 'You have saved the lives of five thousand children and we shall never forget this.' Dennis and I felt this was probably a little exaggerated, but appreciated the offer of free holidays in the Harz mountains in better times to come, an offer I am sorry to say I never actually took up.

In September the Section was moved at short notice. The team were very reluctant to leave the area as there was still a great need and we felt we would be letting the local German authorities down at a very difficult time. Although we protested at the proposed move, the British Red Cross HQ in Vlotho were adamant and they were proved to be right in their difficult decision.

Under the treaty arrangements agreed at the Yalta conference[41], and later at Potsdam, areas of eastern Germany were ceded to Poland, to compensate for the land they were obliged to give to Russia, further to the east, and the German population was expelled. At the time of writing the world has been horrified at the events unfolding in Kosovo, where in very cruel circumstances, about a million ethnic Albanians have been expelled. The term 'ethnic cleansing' had not been invented, but 1945–1946 saw on a large scale what we have seen in Kosovo. During one of the century's most bitter winters between ten and twelve million people were driven out of their towns and villages. Tragically, some two million died on the freezing trek to the four allied zones of occupation. Not wishing to stay in the eastern zone of Germany occupied by the Russian Army, millions continued travelling westwards and flooded into the British zone. In pitiable conditions, with industry laid waste, vast devastation of housing and buildings of all kinds, communications non-existent, agriculture in a poor state, and children already starving in areas like the Ruhr, Germany had to absorb some eight million fellow Germans. All this made few headlines: with Nazi atrocities fresh in people's minds there was not much pity for these German victims. A notable exception was Victor Gollancz and his 'Save Europe Now' campaign.

Many hundreds of thousands were guided to what was considered to be the less damaged areas of Schleswig-Holstein, northwards from Hamburg towards the frontier with Denmark. Our BRC Section was based in Lübeck on the Baltic Sea, but operated in several areas north of the city as far as Eutin. The immediate centre of the town was badly damaged, but surrounding suburbs were hardly touched, and even some shops and cafés were open.

In some areas of Schleswig-Holstein the expellees had nearly doubled the size of the population in a few weeks and there was little or no accommodation for them. It was estimated that in the town of Lübeck alone, enforced billeting, which required one family to a room in private houses, had absorbed some sixty thousand refugees, with another fifteen thousand in very temporary camps. In the whole district were another

A view of Hamburg-Wandsbek in spring 1947

one hundred and fifty thousand. I never did discover the figures for the whole of Schleswig-Holstein outside our area of responsibility.

Camps had been set up on bomb-damaged sites and other spaces in the town, but conditions were appalling in these hastily constructed sheds. No light, no piped water, little fuel, no glass just canvas over the windows, leaking roofs, no drainage or sewerage systems. They became centres of infection and unrest. Involvement in the 'black' market became a way of life, and there was much theft. There was a street market where if you had something stolen you could often find it on one of the stalls and buy it back!

This invasion was much resented by the indigenous population. I wrote home on 29 September, 'but what can you expect from people who have been kicked out of their homes in the "new" Poland with only what they can carry and made to walk hundreds of miles, underfed and often attacked and robbed as they went?' (Many in fact found some rail transport of sorts.) 'They are entirely taken up with their own survival at the moment, but unless conditions are improved they could become a real destabilising factor in the "new" Germany.' For more than a generation the German expellees' organisations campaigned for the right to return to their homes.

We found groups housed in every conceivable building in the area, from farm barns to disused petrol filling stations, putting an impossible burden on the local German authorities. We were able to help a little by discovering materials and tools and getting them released so that the refugees could try to better their conditions. On one occasion we crossed over into the Russian zone, which was strictly forbidden, as we had noticed two large Nissen-type huts that were clearly unused. We had a small party of German workers with us who proceeded to dismantle the huts as quickly as possible. Unfortunately, we were disturbed in this work by two Russian soldiers with their machine guns slung round their necks. However, they proved to be quite amicable after a packet or two of cigarettes were offered, and we were able to transport the huts back to the British zone where they were quickly erected again and put to use as more accommodation.

During the very hard winter of 1946–7, when even the Baltic Sea froze over, the position of the refugees became dire, and on our rounds we despaired to find that people had died overnight from the cold. With the coming of the spring their condition gradually began to improve and it proved possible to raise the food ration in the summer.

I finally returned home to England on 25 July 1947, where I took up work with the medical publisher and bookseller H.K. Lewis & Co. Ltd in London. I was married to Renate in the Friends Meeting House in Welwyn Garden City on 10 July 1948.

CHAPTER 8

Reflections

Among the letters to me from the German helpers, one respondent wrote that in her opinion Sandbostel was a camp for foreign workers not a concentration camp. This is a misunderstanding. Some of the inmates may at one time have been foreign workers, but all had been transferred under horrific conditions from the concentration camp at Neuengamme, near Hamburg. More remained in the camp at Neuengamme, but fared no better. With the Allied armies approaching from the west, east and south, the German authorities transported thousands of the inmates northwards and put them aboard three ships in Lübeck Bay. It is not clear what their ultimate intention was. Unfortunately, the RAF, mistaking the ships for military transports, bombed and sank all three on 3 May 1945. There were very few survivors. The incident is considered among the worst maritime disasters of the twentieth century, far surpassing the sinking of the *Titanic*, where some fifteen hundred people were lost. On the largest ship, the *Cap Arcona*, 4650 drowned, on the *Thielbeck* another 2750, and further hundreds on the third boat.[42] Later in the autumn of 1946, while I was working from Lübeck, I saw from the coast, near

Scharbeutz, the upturned hull of one of these ships far out in the bay. Local people still spoke of bodies being occasionally washed ashore.

As described in an earlier chapter, the political prisoners at Sandbostel had come from all walks of life, but they were in the end just human beings who had been taken by force from their homes. If the prisoners of war in the camp next door could be fed in some way, then so could those in the 'political prisoners' compound. These people had been put in the camp to die. Sandbostel was not an extermination camp in the sense that Auschwitz and others had been, there were no gas chambers or ovens, but the policy of deliberate neglect had resulted in very similar conditions. In some sources it has been referred to as a 'punishment' camp, but it was in all respects a concentration camp.

Although in the immediate situation I had little time to think of these things, I experienced an overpowering feeling of the enormity of the horror I was confronting and I wondered how such things could come about. I believe we all have the capacity for evil. None of us knows how we would have behaved under Nazi rule. But I know also that each of us has the capacity for good, the ability to recognise the human being in the stranger. How was it that every day somebody had stood in those wooden towers looking down on people dying and crying out for help? How was it that people had fired guns at those starving people trying to raid the kitchen for food? How as a conscientious objector could I reconcile those dreadful deeds?

When I read my letters home from Sandbostel after 52 years I was surprised at their calm and matter-of-factness, because this is not how I recall it. I remember being in a turmoil – horrified, stunned and angry. For a moment I felt like leaving the FAU and returning home to join the Army. However, I was quickly persuaded by my colleagues that although this was a not unnatural feeling it was only a gut reaction, and on reflection to leave would be a decision I would come to regret. In any case it was hardly practical and would be a rather irrelevant gesture since the war was soon to be over and they assured me I was more use where I was. I was soon immersed in the desperate needs of others, and my colleagues were proved to be right, for in the end I think the experience and its awfulness came to strengthen my pacifism.

This kind of reaction was not uncommon among those rescuers first entering the Camp. Captain Robert Barer, referred to earlier, was an RAMC doctor attached to 94 Light AA Regiment, who went in with the infantry assault boats over the river Oste and observed the battle for the liberation of the Camp. He wrote in a letter on 3 May:

> I shall never forget Sandbostel. It was much smaller than Belsen but the individual suffering was the same. I laughed at some of the things the papers said about Belsen but now I would believe anything – absolutely anything. The SS are just not human, they must be exterminated. It would be far better to kill a few thousand innocent ones than allow a single one of them to escape.

This was obviously written in the heat of the moment, an instant reaction to unbelievable horror. He went on to write, 'I forced the German Commandant of the PoW camp to go round the political camp with me. [The SS had not permitted those German guards administering the PoW camp to enter the political camp.] And he said, "I must confess that at this moment I am ashamed to be German." I don't really think they knew what went on in these places.' Captain Barer was keen to see that as many Germans as possible should be made aware of the atrocities. On 12 May he wrote in another letter:

> I had the good fortune to be able to take a mixed party of German Naval, Army and civilian medical officers round Sandbostel yesterday. They have done a good job but the political prisoners compound is by no means cleared and there are still unpleasant sights, rows of corpses and so on. They have been able to get about 2000 into a hospital after delousing (done mostly by German nurses and women specially imported). The hospital alone is bad enough. Typhus is still emerging and there are over 200 cases (known). This was the fourth time I'd been round the political camp and each time I've seen some fresh horror. It's terrible to think even after this time we haven't been able to help them all. I think it did the Germans an immense amount of good. Even the doubters were convinced.

On the 30 May he wrote: 'The final number of typhus cases at Sandbostel was over 800, and cases are now appearing in the surrounding villages.'

An earlier incident shows Captain Barer to have been a humane and kindly man. His unit had reached the Rhine in March, and he made his first contact with German civilians, whose 'plight is desperate as nearly every house has been damaged'. He tended an old man in a cellar with 14 other people: 'as I went I heard a young girl say: "You see, they are good people. They are not as we have been told." I'm afraid I felt like crying – in fact I did afterwards. The trouble is that it's always the wrong people who suffer in war – not the really guilty ones.' Captain Barer, as described earlier, was the first British officer to enter Sandbostel, and was later awarded the Military Cross for his exploits. Back in civilian life he later became Professor of Human Biology and Anatomy at the University of Sheffield. He died in 1989. All his letters of his time in the RAMC make fascinating and informative reading and are now held in the Department of Documents at the Imperial War Museum in London. Most have now been collected and published as a book.[43]

The initial reaction among the Germans brought in to clear up the Camp was equally dramatic. Elfie Walther, a high-school girl from Delmenhorst, wrote in her diary on 2 May:

> Nobody at home would believe us if we told them about it. I couldn't stop thinking about how we loved the Führer. Everything he told us was a lie. What is this thing that was called National Socialism? We always thought it was something beautiful and noble. Why is everything so cruel. Why do they kill innocent, helpless people? One can't treat one's enemies like that! It is incomprehensible. Last night I finished with everything that I used to believe was good. People are vile pigs – all of them, including me. And there is meant to be a God? And he allows this to happen? How can we apologise.[44]

One can only guess at the mental torment of this young girl.

It has only been since I thought about putting this book together that I have began to realise that the experience of clearing up Sandbostel has been with me most of my life, albeit subconsciously, and that somehow I was going to be the better for putting it down on paper. My main regret is that after all these years I have not been able to trace any of the ex-inmates, but maybe none still live. It would not be surprising if the survivors of the concentration camps have had a shorter than average life span owing to the deprivations they suffered.

I would like to end this book with an extract from a letter to me in May 1997 from Enno Huchting, in answer to my notice in the *Weser-Kurier*. Although only a schoolboy at the time and not involved in the rescue operation at Sandbostel, he wanted to be of help to me with the book, and sent me maps, photographs of the camp as it is today and much other useful information. He wrote:

> I am writing to you because I still feel the wounded pain of being a citizen of a country whose fellow men and women set up and operated these death camps. In 1972 I saw Auschwitz, but it was an inexplicably long time after the war before I searched out the memorials in my own area – Neuengamme, Bergen-Belsen, the U-boat bunkers at Bremen and now Sandbostel.

On a cold rainy day this March I drove to the village of Sandbostel, which is still small and isolated. I walked through the large memorial place which was dark with many overgrown trees and bushes. I was very surprised to see such a large number of graves. I knew little of Sandbostel and had not appreciated how large the camp must have been at the time. At the memorial place there was no indication as to where the camp had been. I walked away over the fields and then back to the village. Taking another road out of the village I saw among some notice boards a small sign with the words 'Camp Church'. It was still raining, I met only three other people, very little seemed to be going on. I went further and came to a little church, beyond which a narrow path led into some more bushes, sand dunes and fields. Then I saw seven barracks still in the state they had been in when they had been left all those years ago. They are silent witnesses to that terrible time. A place where one can only imagine how human beings vegetated there, human beings who were already broken by hunger, overwork and contempt. I walked across the fields along the fence to see all the barracks. A deep shudder passed through me. I turned and walked back to the village deep in thought.

Epilogue

On 28 January 1998 a small Documentation and Memorial Centre for Sandbostel Camp was opened in the nearby town of Bremervörde, perhaps a little ironically in the same building that was once used for a time by the area Nazi Party. The Centre is in Grosser Platz 4, 27432 Bremervörde, and is open on Mondays and Wednesdays from 9 am to 2 pm. It is run and used as an office by the Sandbostel Memorial Association, although the chairman, Dr Dietmar Kohlrausch, says they are still seeking staff. The Association was formed in the early 1990s but has had little financial or moral support from the local authorities, although the Secretary, Dr Klaus Volland, is released from some of his teaching responsibilities at the Bremervörde Gymnasium to enable him to carry out work connected with the Camp memorial site. The official opening of the Centre has raised the question of its maintenance, and the Association would like to ensure that at some point a suitable memorial stone is erected directly on the Camp site. This will require considerable finance, and at the time of writing there is a proposal to approach authorities at Federal, Provincial and local levels about this.

The newly opened Centre has only two rooms, nothing on the scale of the arrangements provided at Bergen-Belsen. The first room has some display panels and two models of the Camp, but as yet no articles to record the daily life in the Camp. The second room is used for archive material and also acts as an office.

There are still a small number of barracks standing at the Camp, but only a small stone at the entrance to the site which indicates that a PoW camp existed there from 1939 to 1945. No mention is made here of the concentration camp victims. The mass graves were exhumed by the Graves Commission under French supervision, between 1953 and 1956, and the bodies reburied at the Cemetery some 2 km away. At the Cemetery, where both PoWs and political prisoners are buried, there is a large memorial comprising three pillars with the inscription: 'Your sacrifice – our obligation – Peace'. This was erected in 1956 to replace a Soviet memorial just for the Russian PoWs buried there, which was blown up with official approval during the Cold War.

After liberation the Camp site had a varied history, although many barracks had been destroyed. Until 1948 some SS and other National Socialist functionaries were imprisoned there. Then from 1952 to 1960 the barracks served as a transit camp for young people fleeing from East Germany. Since 1974 a small industrial area has developed. Firms are using parts of the site which had not been converted back to

Seven barracks buildings still standing on the site of the former concentration camp at Sandbostel, left in the same condition as when the Camp was abandoned over fifty years ago. These could well be the barracks used as a 'clean' improvised hospital. The 'dirty' barracks were mostly burnt down. March 1997. In 1945 it was bare heathland with no trees. Photo: Enno Huchting

farmland; among these are a timber dealer, a local authority road repair service and a riding school which has taken over the former camp kitchen. There are about twenty buildings used in this way and Dr Klaus Volland points out it is historically unique in that the Camp's main structures at least have been preserved. He hopes this will be recognised and that the buildings will be kept as monuments to a period of history that should not be forgotten. Dr Volland offers guided tours of the Camp area.

[Opposite] Annual service of remembrance at the memorial stones for political prisoners and prisoners of war in the cemetery about 2 km from the site of Sandbostel Camp.
[Above] Three German students give readings during the annual service of remembrance by the memorial stones. Photos: Enno Huchting

The Religious Society of Friends and the FAU

The Religious Society of Friends (Quakers)

The Quaker movement arose in the mid-seventeenth century in a deeply divided society where religion was of passionate interest. Translations of the Bible in English had been available from the middle of the sixteenth century, so for about a hundred years people had slowly but increasingly been able to read for themselves without having to have the scriptures mediated to them through 'educated' ministers of religion. In the 1650s a group of men and women led by George Fox (1624–1961) came together to revive what they saw as 'primitive Christianity'. They could not accept that the forms of Christianity they observed around them were in keeping with the teachings of Jesus. They travelled the length and breadth of Britain meeting with groups of people who were seeking a way to live more simply and truly the Christian life. The message spread across the Atlantic, and then around the world.

Today, British Quakerism has developed into 'a group of insights, attitudes and practices which together form a way of life, rather than a dogma or creed. It rests on a conviction that by looking into their inmost hearts people can have a direct communion with their Creator. This experience cannot ultimately be described in words, but Quakers base their whole lives on it.'[45]

> In their meetings for worship Quakers do not sing hymns or use set prayers, but wait on God together in silence. Out of this silence occasionally someone may speak briefly, or pray, or read from the Bible or other religious work Quakers often express themselves in Christian terms, but many different kinds of religious experience may be brought before God in the silent group.[46]

Quakers have always maintained that their inward worship turns them out into the world and that their faith should show in the way they live their lives. Their belief in 'that of God' in everyone has led them to take up causes which support people rejected or neglected by society:

> Early Quakers took to heart the revolution begun by Jesus with its emphasis on loving relationships, and soon concluded that taking up arms for any cause whatsoever was incompatible with this way of life. As well as opposing war, Quakers have tried to bring about peaceful solutions by mediation and reconciliation. They have struggled to relieve poverty and combat injustice which are both the causes and the results of warfare.[47]

What is seen as Quaker work is really of two kinds. Those activities with which the whole Society of Friends can unite are organised through central departments and committees and become the corporate and official expression of the Society's life. However, there have been many other pieces of work initiated and sponsored by individual Friends or groups for which the Society did not take official responsibility. The Friends Ambulance Unit was in this category.

The Friends Ambulance Unit – First World War

The FAU was started by a number of individual Quakers at the outbreak of the First World War. 'Among these was a young man later to achieve fame as the Nobel laureate Philip Noel Baker. This vigorous young Friend and athletics blue, Olympic medallist and President of the Cambridge Union, later became a socialist politician, peer of the realm and lifelong campaigner for disarmament.'[48] The FAU was self-governing and was constitutionally and financially independent, although it followed a general Quaker line. It was therefore free to make its own arrangements with military authorities and in effect became a form of alternative service for conscientious objectors, gathering in the process numbers of non-Quakers. Because of the co-operation with military authorities there was from time to time tension between the FAU and official Quaker bodies. However, as the work of the FAU developed it came to be regarded by most Friends as being as much in the tradition of Quaker service as anything that was done officially, and 'in spite of some uneasiness, Yearly Meeting (the corporate decision-making body of British Friends) in 1916 cordially endorsed a proposal that some Friend or Friends should convey our desire for their welfare and give whatever spiritual help and encouragement is possible.'[49]

The FAU ran hospitals in France and Belgium, worked on hospital trains and ships and helped to meet the emergency needs of civilians and refugees. The FAU was laid down in 1919. It had been served by over a thousand people, predominately men, in Britain and abroad. It was reckoned that some seventy per cent were Quakers. 'At the end of the war, 640 members were serving abroad, 440 others in the general service section were doing work of national importance at home (mainly educational, welfare, or agricultural work), and 300 were working in hospitals.'[50] Like the nation at large, it had its roll of honour. Twenty-one of its members died on active service.

The Friends Ambulance Unit – Second World War

With war clouds gathering again and talk of compulsory military service being introduced, members of the FAU from the First World War held a reunion in October 1938. As a result a committee, including Paul Cadbury, Arnold Rowntree and John Harvey, was set up to consider whether the FAU should be reconstituted. Within a month of the outbreak of war in September 1939 the first training camp had assembled. The FAU had been re-established for men of military age who 'shared the Quaker view of peace and war' and had been conditionally registered as conscientious objectors (official exemption to military service) by a tribunal. During the following six years five thousand men applied to join, of whom some 1300 were accepted. Seventeen members lost their lives. This time women were welcomed from 1941 and by 1945 ninety-seven had served.

FAU members formed their own administration and raised their own funds and decided what work should be undertaken. It was all very democratic. Relations with the official bodies of the Religious Society of

Friends were less difficult than in the First World War, but there was early criticism among some Quakers about the use of the word 'Friends' in the title of the FAU, and considerable unease about the Unit's relations with the military and the wearing of khaki uniform in war zones. It was felt that the witness of those conscientious objectors who took a more absolutist line would be compromised. When Friends Relief Service workers were finally able to enter Europe towards the end of the war they were able to negotiate the wearing of a distinctive grey uniform. Although there was more recognition of the work of the FAU among Friends than in the First World War, the FAU retained its independence and was solely responsible for the work it undertook; this time it did report to Yearly Meeting. In 1942 the Home Section of the FAU merged with the official Friends War Victims Committee to form the Friends War Relief Service, later to be known more simply as the Friends Relief Service.

All those accepted into membership of the FAU went through a basic training camp of about six to eight weeks. This experience of fending for oneself and getting on with others as a team proved invaluable. Apart from First Aid and nursing certificate courses, some physical training and even route marching was included, and everyone took a turn at catering and hygiene. Most then went on to gain experience in hospitals, nursing on wards and casualty departments, and even in operating theatres and X-ray departments. Many others then had instruction in vehicle driving and maintenance, and courses on civilian relief work.

At home the FAU worked in air raid shelters in London and other large cities during the Blitz, ran rest centres for bombed-out families, acted as human guinea pigs for medical research in several spheres like malaria and scabies, and worked as orderlies in over eighty hospitals. The main focus, however, was on work abroad, and as the war spread worldwide the FAU became widely dispersed. By the end of 1946 overseas sections had served in Austria, Belgium, Finland, Germany, Greece, Italy, the Netherlands, Norway, Yugoslavia, Egypt, Ethiopia, Lebanon, Libya, Syria, Tunisia, China and India. The work had included medical and surgical teams with British and Free French forces in various war zones, medical work in Ethiopia, driving medical supplies in China, relief work during famine and floods in Bengal, and relief and refugee work in Europe and much more.

This description of the work of the FAU has necessarily been extremely brief, but readers wishing to know more are referred in particular to two books: *Friends Ambulance Unit: The Story of the FAU in the Second World War 1939–1946*, by A. Tegla Davies (Allen & Unwin, 1947, now out of print), and *Pacifists in Action: The Experience of the Friends Ambulance Unit in the Second World War* by Lyn Smith (York: Sessions, 1998).

In 1947, through its representative bodies, the American Friends Service Committee and the Friends Service Council of London, the Religious Society of Friends was awarded the Nobel Peace Prize. Although not specifically mentioned it was generally accepted that the contribution of the FAU was included along with all the other work of the Society for peace and reconciliation.

The FAU formally closed on 30 June 1946, but was succeeded by the

FAU Post-War Service, which later became the FAU International Service until it in turn came to an end in 1959, when conscription was ended. Its story can be found in *FAU: The Third Generation. Friends Ambulance Unit Post War Service and International Service 1946–1959* by Roger Bush (York: Sessions, 1998).

Readers wishing to know more about Quaker belief and practice should write to: Quaker Home Service, Religious Society of Friends, Friends House, 173–177 Euston Road, London NW1 2BJ, for a free book and information.

Notes

1. This report is part of the collection of papers of Professor H.C. McLaren, MD, FRCS, who as a Major in the RAMC was a Surgical Specialist with 10 CCS at the time of the liberation of Sandbostel Camp. Although not quoted in this book, his own account gives his initial impression of the horrific circumstances in the Camp. His papers are unpublished, but may be consulted in the Department of Documents at the Imperial War Museum in London.

2. Vera Brittain, *Humiliation with Honour* (London: Andrew Dakers, 1942, out of print).

3. George Fox, 1651. See *Quaker faith and practice* (London: Religious Society of Friends,1995): para. 24. n1.

4. Details of these experiments may also be found in Kenneth Mellanby, *Human Guinea Pigs*, London: Gollancz, 1947, (out of print).

5. For much of the information in this chapter I am indebted to A. Tegla Davies: *Friends Ambulance Unit: The Story of the FAU in the Second World War 1939–1946*, (London: Allen & Unwin, 1947). Sadly this informative book has been out of print for many years.

6. Davies, op.cit., p. 424

7. Davies, op.cit., p. 427

8. Davies, op.cit., p. 429

9. 205 (R) Military Government Detachment War Diary. WO 205/ 1034 (London: Public Record Office).

10. Richard Wainwright, 'Relief Work in Displaced Persons Camps' in *Over to You*, August 1945, a journal of the British Red Cross Commission.

11. For a description of the work undertaken by an FAU team rebuilding social and spiritual bonds in Germany from mid-1945 to mid-1946 see Grigor McClelland, *Embers of War:Letters from a Quaker Relief Worker in War-torn Germany* (London: British Academic Press, I.B. Tauris & Co. Ltd, 1997).

12. For much of the factual and statistical information in this chapter I am indebted to *The Medical History of the Second World War; The Army Medical Services (Campaigns), vol. iv, North-West Europe*, edited by F.A.E. Crew (London: HMSO, 1962), pp. 498–505.

13. Captain Robert Barer, MC, RAMC, 'Report on Sandbostel Concentration Camp, 1945' in *One Young Man and Total War – from Normandy to Concentration Camp: A Doctor's Letters Home.* (Durham: Pentland Press, 1998), pp.276–285.

14. Hugh Johnes, Memoirs. Unpublished, in author's possession.

15. Crew, op. cit., pp. 498–499.

16. Crew, op. cit., pp. 499–500.

17. 168 Light Field Ambulance War Diary. WO 177 882 (London: Public Record Office).

18. 205 (R) Mil Gov Det War Diary, op.cit.

19. Crew, op.cit., p. 502.

20. Crew, op.cit., p. 500.

21. Crew, op.cit., p. 501.

22. Crew, op.cit., p. 503.

23. Hugh Johnes, op.cit.

24. As far as I was aware no bombs were dropped on the Camp from the German planes and the artillery shells all landed in the fields short of the Camp.

25. Crew, op.cit., p. 500.

26. Crew, op.cit., p. 500.

27. I have been unable to trace this report or who Colonel Evans was or to which unit he was attached.

28. Crew, op.cit., p. 503.

29. Crew, op.cit., p. 502.

30. Gordon Taylor, Memoirs. Unpublished, in author's possession.

31. Gordon Taylor, op.cit.

32. Crew, op.cit., p. 504.

33. 168 Light Field Ambulance War Diary, op. cit.

34. Barer, op.cit., p. 294.

35. Crew, op.cit., p. 504.

36. Crew, op.cit., p. 505.

37. Crew, op.cit., p. 505.

38. Werner Borgsen and Klaus Volland, *Stalag XB Sandbostel: zur Geschichte eines Kriegsgefangenen-und KZ-Auffanglagers in Norddeutschland 1939–1945*. Bremen: Edition Temmen, 1991, in German, p. 210. A copy of this book was sent to me by Enno Huchting in which he had written: 'This book is for Clifford Barnard and his comrades, who as young men had to witness how cruel Germans treated people from foreign lands.'

39. M.C. Carey, 'The Gradual return to normality', in *Over to You*, August 1945.

40. 205 Mil Gov Det War Diary, op.cit.

41. A conference held in February 1945 at Yalta, on the south coast of the Crimea in Russia, between Churchill, Roosevelt and Stalin to make plans for the final defeat and occupation of Germany. The Potsdam agreement arose out of a later conference held at Potsdam, near Berlin, in July 1945, between Churchill and Attlee for Great Britain, Truman for the USA, and Stalin for the Soviet Union.

42. Source: National Maritime Museum.

43. See note 13.

44. Ulrike Jordan, ed. *Conditions of Surrender: British and Germans Witness the End of the War* (London: Tauris Academic Studies, 1997), p. 107.

45. Richard Allen, *The Quaker Way*, leaflet issued by Quaker Home Service, London.

46. Allen, op.cit.

47. *Who are the Quakers?*, leaflet issued by Quaker Home Service, London.

48. John Punshon, *Portrait in Grey: A Short History of the Quakers* (London: Quaker Home Service, 1984), p. 233.

49. Sydney Bailey, *Peace is a Process* (London: Quaker Home Service, 1993), p. 46.

50. Bailey, op.cit., p. 46.

Acknowledgements

Mainly for the purposes of facts and figures I have quoted from *The Medical History of the Second World War. The Army Medical Services (Campaigns) Vol. iv North-West Europe*, edited by F. A.E. Crew (HMSO, 1962), this Crown copyright is reproduced with the permission of the controller of Her Majesty's Stationery Office.

I am grateful to Dr Gwenda Barer for her permission to quote from the letters of her late husband, Captain R. Barer MC, held in the Department of Documents at the Imperial War Museum in London, and to I.B. Tauris & Co. Ltd for permission to use the extract from Elfie Walther's diary in their book *Conditions of Surrender* edited by Ulrike Jordan.

I have also quoted extensively from the diary of Dennis Wickham. This was passed to Gordon Taylor by Dennis's widow following his death some ten years ago, saying she would be happy for it to be used in any way that might be thought appropriate. I have not been able to trace her present address so I have been unable to seek her specific permission to use extracts in this book, but I am sure from my fond memory of Dennis that he would be delighted for this to happen. The hand-written diary is now deposited in the Library at Friends House in London with other FAU archive material.

I am deeply grateful to Gordon Taylor, Hugh Johnes and George Champion, members of 2 FAU at the time of Sandbostel, for replying with much useful information to my letter seeking their help. Also to Ilse Schröder, Maria von Reinken, Marianne Martens, Rosemarie Kirmse, Ingebörg Wark, Anne Loesche and Hannelore Langbein for responding to my notice in the *Weser-Kurier*. Their often moving contributions have added much to the book giving it a wider perspective. Also especially to Enno Huchting, for his interest in my book; he visited the site of the Camp and cemetery, and sent me photographs, maps and much other useful information.

I am so grateful to my parents whose foresight all those years ago in preserving my letters home made this book possible. I would also like to thank Stephen Walton of the Department of Documents at the Imperial War Museum who guided me towards many valuable sources of information, and to Graham Heath and Renate Barnard for translating the German letters.

In a few instances it has not been possible to discover where to write for permission. In these cases I hope authors and others will forgive me for using their words without permission.

I am indebted to so many, not least those who encouraged me to write in the first instance, especially Jim Pym, and to those who read the book in draft and made many helpful comments, in particular Alison Leonard, Elisabeth Salisbury, Enno Huchting, and members of the Quaker Home Service Literature Committee.

I gratefully acknowledge the Trustees of the Imperial War Museum for their permission to include the official photographs of Sandbostel Camp from their Photographic Archive Department. I have to thank Enno Huchting for allowing me to use his photographs of Sandbostel Camp as it is today and for those he took at a memorial meeting at the present cemetery. I have included a number of photographs of the Friends Ambulance Unit team. Some of these were taken by George Champion, but I no longer know the photographer of the others and so have been unable to seek their permission. I am sorry I have been unable to do this. However, I warmly thank all those concerned.